COMMON CORE ACHIEVE

Mastering Essential Test Readiness Skills

GED® Test Exercise Book
SOCIAL STUDIES

Bothell, WA • Chicago, IL • Columbus, OH • New York, NY

GED®, GED TESTING SERVICE®, and GED PLUS® are registered trademarks owned by American Council on Education ("ACE"). This material is not endorsed or approved by ACE or the GED Testing Service LLC.

MHEonline.com

Copyright © 2015 McGraw-Hill Education

All rights reserved. No part of this publication may be reproduced or distributed in any form or by any means, or stored in a database or retrieval system, without the prior written consent of McGraw-Hill Education, including, but not limited to, network storage or transmission, or broadcast for distance learning.

Send all inquiries to:
McGraw-Hill Education
8787 Orion Place
Columbus, OH 43240

ISBN: 978-0-02-135573-0
MHID: 0-02-135573-8

Printed in the United States of America.

1 2 3 4 5 6 7 8 9 RHR 17 16 15 14

Table of Contents

To the Student v

Chapter 1 Government

1.1	Types of Government	1
1.2	American Constitutional Democracy	5
1.3	Structure of American Government	9

Chapter 2 Civics

2.1	Individual Rights and Responsibilities	13
2.2	Political Parties, Campaigns, and Elections	17
2.3	Contemporary Public Policy	21

Chapter 3 American History: Revolutionary War Through Civil War

3.1	American Revolution	25
3.2	A New Nation	29
3.3	Civil War and Reconstruction	33
3.4	European Settlement and Population of the Americas	37

Chapter 4 American History: World War I Through Modern Times

4.1	World War I	41
4.2	World War II	45
4.3	The Cold War	49
4.4	Societal Changes	53
4.5	Foreign Policy in the 21st Century	57

Chapter 5 Fundamentals of Economics

5.1	Markets, Monopolies, and Competition	61
5.2	The Factors of Production	65
5.3	Profits and Productivity	69
5.4	Specialization and Comparative Advantage	73

Chapter 6 Microeconomics and Macroeconomics

6.1	Microeconomics	77
6.2	Macroeconomics and Government Policy	81
6.3	Macroeconomics, the GDP, and Price Fluctuation	85

Chapter 7   Economics and History

7.1	Major Economic Events	89
7.2	The Relationship between Politics and Economics	93
7.3	The Scientific and Industrial Revolutions	97

Chapter 8   Consumer Credit

8.1	Savings and Banking	101
8.2	Types of Credit	105
8.3	Consumer Credit Laws	109

Chapter 9   Societal Development

9.1	Development of Ancient Civilizations	113
9.2	Nationhood and Statehood	117
9.3	Human Activity and the Environment	121

Chapter 10   Borders Between People and Nations

10.1	Concepts of Region and Place	125
10.2	Natural and Cultural Diversity	129
10.3	Population Trends and Issues	133
	Answer Key	137

To the Student

Congratulations! If you are using this book, it means that you are taking a key step toward achieving an important new goal for yourself. You are preparing to take the GED® Test in order to earn your high school diploma, one of the most important steps in the pathway toward career, educational, and lifelong well-being and success.

Common Core Achieve: Mastering Essential Test Readiness Skills is designed to help you learn or strengthen the skills you will need when you take the GED® Test. The Social Studies Exercise Book provides you with additional practice of the key concepts and core skills and practices required for success on test day and beyond.

How to Use This Book

This book is designed to follow the same lesson structure as the Core Student Module. Each lesson in the Social Studies Exercise Book is broken down into the same sections covering key concepts as the core module, with a page or more devoted to the topics covered in each section. Each lesson contains at least one Test-Taking Tip, which helps you prepare for a test by giving you hints such as how to approach certain question types, or strategies such as how to eliminate unnecessary information. At the back of this book, you will find the answer key for each lesson. Not only are the answers provided, but there are also rationales for each multiple-choice question that gives explanations why each answer choice is correct or incorrect. If you get an answer incorrect, please return to the appropriate lesson and section in either the online or print Core Student Module to review the specific content.

About the GED® Social Studies Test

The GED® Social Studies Test assesses across four major content areas: civics and government, United States History, economics, and geography. Each question on the test is aligned to a Social Studies Practice and Social Studies Content Topic in order to gauge fluency, content understanding, and reasoning skills. Multiple item types are used on the test including multiple choice, fill-in-the-blank, drop-down, drag-and-drop, extended response, and hotspot. Many item types utilize primary sources, graphs, tables, maps, or other information presented visually.

The GED® Social Studies Test assesses across the Webb's Depth of Knowledge spectrum, asking students to answer questions that range from recall questions (DOK 1) to strategic thinking questions (DOK 3). The test assesses approximately 20% of its items at the DOK 1 level (recall), and 80% of its items at the DOK 2 (application of concepts) and DOK 3 (strategic thinking) levels.

Item Types

The GED® test consists of a variety of question types, including multiple choice, fill-in-the-blank, drop-down, drag-and-drop, extended response, and hot spot. To prepare you for the GED® test, the Social Studies Exercise Book models those computer-based question types in a print format to help familiarize you with what you will experience on test day.

Multiple Choice Items

The multiple-choice question is the most common type of question you will encounter. Each multiple-choice question will contain 4 answer choices, of which there will be only one correct answer. When encountering a multiple-choice question, look for any possible answers that cannot be correct based on the information given. You may also see extraneous information in the question that is used in the answer choices. Identify and eliminate this information so you can focus on the relevant information to answer the question.

3. People who were opposed to slavery were known as

A. abolitionists.

B. slave traders.

C. confederates.

D. unionists.

Fill-in-the-blank (FIB) Items

A fill-in-the-blank item has you either complete a sentence by writing in the number, word, or phrase that completes the sentence, or write in the number, word, or phrase that answers a question. If the blank occurs within a sentence, make sure to not only fill in the blank, but to make sure the sentence makes sense, keeping track of verb tenses when writing text and using appropriate units when writing numbers.

9. By specializing and producing those items for which they had a comparative advantage, separate gun producers and butter producers could together produce _____ total butter and guns.

A. 100

B. 105

C. 110

D. 120

Drop-down Items

The drop-down items are questions that give a drop-down menu within the text with choices to fill in the space to complete the sentence. There can be multiple drop-down items in a text, each with its own set of possible answers. When answering drop-down items, try to eliminate answer choices that are meant as a distraction, including choices with unnecessary information from the text or choices that reuse information from a previous drop-down item. Within this book, these items are simulated by showing an expanded drop down menu from which the correct answer can be selected.

5. Company A and Company B both make mops and brooms. If Company A can make more mops and brooms than Company B, it has a higher [1] Select... ▼ than Company B. Because Company A makes more mops than brooms, it wants to [2] Select... ▼ in mops.

[1] Select... ▼

A. monopoly

B. specialization

C. absolute advantage

D. comparative advantage

[2] Select... ▼

A. monopoly

B. specialize

C. absolute advantage

D. comparative advantage

To the Student

Drag-and-drop Items

A drag-and-drop activity is an item type where you are required to drag text or images and drop them in a specific place. Examples of drag-and-drop items include categorizing or ordering events, dates, or data. For a drag-and-drop item, you will be given multiple items that need to be dragged, called draggables. Each draggable will need to classified, categorized, or matched to the appropriate location, or target. Within this book, these items are simulated through writing each draggable in the appropriate target area.

12. In the chart below, identify the characteristics of the Articles of Confederation and the Constitution.

   | A. Passing laws requires approval of 9 of 13 states | B. Government divided into three branches | C. Representation based on population House of Representatives |
   | D. Each state gets one vote in Senate | E. Congress has no authority to pass taxes | F. Trade regulated by states |

Articles of Confederation	Constitution

Hotspot Items

A hotspot item consists of an image in which there are interactive spots on a graph or another image. This item type is used to select data or points on a map or in a graph, chart, or table to correctly answer a question. Within this book, these items are simulated through circling the correct point or region on the graphic.

10. Write the letter in the circle that correctly corresponds to the date on the timeline below. Then circle the events that had a direct effect on improvements in women's rights.

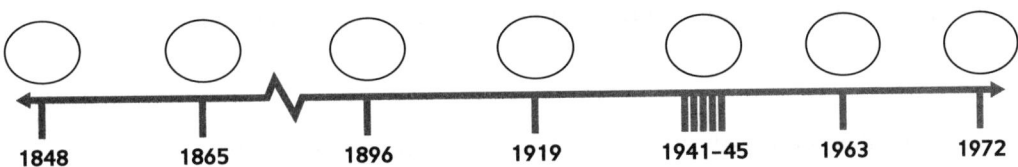

1848   1865   1896   1919   1941–45   1963   1972

   a. passage of the Thirteenth Amendment
   b. publication of Betty Friedan's *The Feminine Mystique*
   c. Seneca Falls Conference
   d. Congress approves the Equal Rights Amendment
   e. World War II
   f. *Plessy v. Ferguson*
   g. passage of the Nineteenth Amendment

Strategies for Test Day

There are many things you should do to prepare for test day, including studying. Other ways to prepare you for the day of the test include preparing physically, arriving early, and recognizing certain strategies to help you succeed during the test. Some of these strategies are listed below.

- **Prepare physically.** Make sure you are rested both physically and mentally the day of the test. Eating a well-balanced meal will also help you concentrate while taking the text. Staying stress-free as much as possible on the day of the test will make you more likely to stayed focused than when you are stressed.

- **Arrive early.** Arrive at the testing center at least 20 minutes before the beginning of the test. Give yourself enough time to get seated and situated in the room. Keep in mind that many testing centers will not admit you if you are late. Other centers only admit test-takers on a first come, first served basis, and so getting there early will help guarantee you a seat on the day of the test.

- **Think positively.** Studies have shown that a positive attitude can help with success, although studying helps even more.

- **Relax during the test.** Stretching and deep breathing can help you relax and refocus. Try doing this a few times during the test, especially if you feel frustrated, anxious, or confused.

- **Read the test directions carefully.** Make sure you understand what the directions are asking you to do and complete the activity appropriately. If you have any questions about the test, or how to answer a specific item type using the computer, ask before the beginning of the test.

- **Know the time limit for each test.** Try to work at a manageable pace. If you have extra time, go back to check your answers and finish any questions you might have skipped.

- **Have a strategy for answering questions.** For each question, read through the question prompt, identifying the important information to answer the question. If you need, reread the information provided as well as any answer choices provided.

- **Don't spend a lot of time on difficult questions.** If you are unsure of the answer to a question, you can click on "Flag for Review" in the upper right corner of the screen. A yellow flag will appear. Continuing with the remaining questions might help you figure out the answer to a difficult question. At the end of the test, you will come to a review screen, where your flagged questions will be marked. If time remains, you can return to those questions.

- **Answer every question on the test.** If you do not know the answer, make your best guess. You will lose points leaving questions unanswered, but making a guess could possibly help you gain points.

Good luck with your studies, and remember: you are here because you have chosen to achieve important and exciting new goals for yourself. Every time you begin working within the materials, keep in mind that the skills you develop in Common Core Achieve: Mastering Essential Test Readiness Skills are not just important for passing the GED® Test; they are keys to lifelong success.

Types of Modern and Historical Governments Lesson 1.1

This lesson will help you understand how governments vary among countries and identify documents that contributed to American democracy. Use it with core lesson 1.1 Types of Modern and Historical Governments to reinforce and apply your knowledge.

Key Concept
Governments within a state, country, or region are responsible for establishing order, providing security, and directing public affairs.

Core Skills & Practices
- Compare Ideas
- Analyze Ideas

Types of Government

Different types of government exist throughout the world at the local, state, and national levels.

Directions: Read the following questions. Then select the correct answer.

1. In which type of government does a king or queen serve as head of state?

    A. democracy

    B. monarchy

    C. oligarchy

    D. parliament

2. Why was the Magna Carta written?

    A. to establish rights for US citizens

    B. to plan for a new government of Virginia

    C. to protect the rights of British citizens

    D. to define the rights of monarchs

3. How is the legislature in the United States similar to the parliament in Canada?

    A. Both contain representatives elected by citizens.

    B. Both contain a Senate and a House of Representatives.

    C. Both are set up by the head of state.

    D. Both have a House of Commons.

4. Authoritarian governments _____

    A. protect the rights of individuals.

    B. derive power from the people.

    C. have all been replaced by democratic governments.

    D. often rely on military power and terror.

Directions: Read the passages below. Than answer questions that follow.

> [B]ut an oligarchy and democracy differ in this from each other, in the poverty of those who govern in the one, and the riches of those who govern in the other; for when the government is in the hands of the rich, be they few or be they more, it is an oligarchy; when it is in the hands of the poor, it is a democracy: but, as we have already said, the one will be always few, the other numerous, but both will enjoy liberty; and from the claims of wealth and liberty will arise continual disputes with each other for the lead in public affairs.
>
> —Aristotle in *A Treatise on Government*
>
> Is it credible that the democracy which has annihilated the feudal system and vanquished kings will respect the citizen and the capitalist? Will it stop now that it has grown so strong and its adversaries so weak? None can say which way we are going, for all terms of comparison are wanting: the equality of conditions is more complete in the Christian countries of the present day than it has been at any time or in any part of the world; so that the extent of what already exists prevents us from foreseeing what may be yet to come.
>
> —Alexis De Tocqueville in *Democracy in America*

5. Read the two excerpts. What are Aristotle and Tocqueville both concerned about regarding democracy?

   A. the poverty of those who govern

   B. the strength of oligarchies

   C. the power of the rich versus the poor

   D. the liberty of Christian countries

6. According to Aristotle, when is a democracy like an oligarchy?

   A. when those in power are poor

   B. when those in power are wealthy

   C. when those in power are in the minority

   D. when those in power are in the majority

7. What is Tocqueville worried about regarding the future of democracy?

   A. that the feudal system will return to Christian nations

   B. that monarchies will replace democratic governments

   C. that democratic governments will overtake the world

   D. that citizens and capitalists will be treated relatively equally

8. How does a dictatorship differ from a constitutional monarchy?

   A. Monarchs have ceremonial power, whereas dictators have absolute power.

   B. Dictators are elected, whereas monarchs are usually born to their position.

   C. Monarchs are elected, whereas dictators seize power by force.

   D. Dictators have to follow a constitution, whereas monarchs have to obey parliament.

Documents That Contributed to the Development of American Democracy

Several historical documents played an important role in the establishment of the US government.

Directions: Read the following questions. Then select the correct answer.

9. Complete the following table with the correct documents. Not all will be used.

Author	Document
British nobles	
Thomas Jefferson	
George Mason	
Founders of US government	

Declaration of Independence	Magna Carta
Mayflower Compact	Bill of Rights
Virginia Declaration of Rights	

  Test-Taking Tip

When answering a drag-and-drop question, it is important to read the question carefully before matching items. Once you are sure you understand the question, carefully read the items to match. First match the items you feel confident you know, then go back and work on the items you are less sure about.

10. Write the correct events in the timeline below.

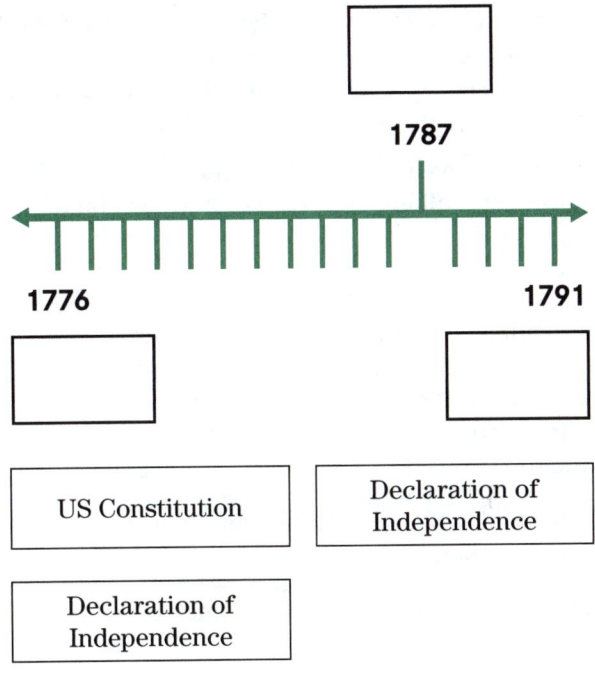

US Constitution

Declaration of Independence

Declaration of Independence

11. Including the Bill of Rights, there are 27 amendments. What can you infer about the inclusion of an amendment process in the Constitution?

   A. The authors of the Constitution realized it was a flawed document that would require revision.

   B. The authors of the Constitution could not agree on the rights to include.

   C. An amendment process was included so the Constitution would be a flexible document and change as society changed.

   D. The amendment process was included because the authors did not want a Constitution that would be changed.

Directions: Read the passage below. Then answer the questions that follow.

> Fifteenth Amendment—The right of citizens of the United States to vote shall not be denied or abridged by the United States or by any State on account of race, color, or previous condition of servitude.
>
> Nineteenth Amendment—The right of citizens of the United States to vote shall not be denied or abridged by the United States or by any State on account of sex.
>
> Twenty-Fourth Amendment—The right of citizens of the United States to vote in any primary or other election for President or Vice President, for electors for President or Vice President, or for Senator or Representative in Congress, shall not be denied or abridged by the United States or any State by reason of failure to pay any poll tax or other tax.
>
> Twenty-Sixth Amendment—The right of citizens of the United States, who are eighteen years of age or older, to vote shall not be denied or abridged by the United States or by any State on account of age.

12. The amendments to the US Constitution are listed in numerical and chronological order. Based on this information, which of the following is true? The right to vote was granted to

A. white women before African American men or women.

B. African American men before women of any race.

C. eighteen-year-old women before eighteen-year-old men.

D. African Americans before they were legally declared citizens.

13. Many citizens who were old enough to serve in the military were angered that they were not old enough to vote. Their protests resulted in which amendment?

A. the Fifteenth Amendment

B. the Nineteenth Amendment

C. the Twenty-Fourth Amendment

D. the Twenty-Sixth Amendment

14. Based on the above amendments, which statement best summarizes the history of voting rights in the United States?

A. Certain groups of citizens choose not to participate in voting for various reasons.

B. Certain groups of citizens use the amendment process to ensure their votes are more important than other groups' votes.

C. Over time, the amendment process has been necessary to protect the voting rights of all citizens.

D. As different groups of citizens have come to the Untied States, they have been granted the right to vote through the amendment process.

15. After gaining independence, Americans were concerned about the new government having too much power. On a separate sheet of paper, write an essay in which you explain the measures taken by the Framers of the Constitution to prevent the government from becoming too powerful. Consider different features of the Constitution and Bill of Rights.

American Constitutional Democracy Lesson 1.2

This lesson will help you understand what led to the Constitutional Convention and how compromises led to constitutional amendments. Use it with core lesson 1.2 American Constitutional Democracy to reinforce and apply your knowledge.

Key Concept
The Constitution was not met with universal approval and had to be changed to get the new American states to approve it.

Core Skills & Practices
- Determine the Relevance of Information
- Read a Bar Graph

The Need for a Constitution

After the Revolutionary War, the first plan of government, the Articles of Confederation, was not strong enough for the new country.

Directions: Read the following questions. Then select the correct answers.

1. Most states included "natural rights" clauses in their constitutions. These were rights that

   A. allowed each citizen to do whatever he or she wanted.

   B. protected a citizen's right to not pay taxes.

   C. established a true democracy in those states.

   D. no government would be allowed to violate.

2. Under constitutionalism, which of the following is true?

   A. The government's power comes from its citizens.

   B. The government's power is based on a set of written rules.

   C. Provisions for change within the government are unnecessary.

   D. The government's power is unlimited.

3. Write a persuasive essay from the position of a delegate to the Second Continental Congress. Congress is debating whether to allow the central government to impose taxes. Take a stand on the issue. On a separate sheet of paper, defend your position. Give specific reasons for your opinion.

4. Match each effect of Shays's Rebellion to the correct cause to complete the chart.

Shays's Rebellion, 1786–1787	
Cause	Effect
The Articles of Confederation did not make provisions for collecting taxes and paying off the nation's war debts. Each state had to collect its own taxes. Many farmers did not have enough money to pay their tax debts.	
Several farmers in Massachusetts, including a Revolutionary War veteran named Daniel Shays, believed they were being treated unfairly and became angry.	
The Articles of Confederation was seen as ineffective because it did not provide a strong central government.	

- courts and tax collectors seized farms as repayment for debt
- farmers took up arms against state governments
- US Constitution drafted and passed as a more effective plan of government

A Nation Built on Compromise

The Constitutional Convention convened in 1787 to rewrite the rules by which the United States would work. The result was the US Constitution.

Directions: Read the following questions. Then select the correct answer.

5. Citizens retain popular sovereignty in a country by which of the following?

   A. taking part in the judicial system as jurors at trials

   B. running for office

   C. voting in federal, state, and local elections

   D. paying taxes at the federal, state, and local levels

6. Which of the following quotes best describes the rule of law?

   A. "The fundamental law of the militia is, that it be created, directed and commanded by the laws, and ever for the support of the laws." —John Adams

   B. "In framing a government which is to be administered by men over men you must first enable the government to control the governed." —James Madison

   C. "For as in absolute governments the King is law, so in free countries the law ought to be king; and there ought to be no other." —Thomas Paine

   D. "A Bill of Rights is what the people are entitled to against every government, and what no just government should refuse." —Thomas Jefferson

Directions: Read the passage below. Then answer the questions that follow.

> Written by James Madison, [Federalist, No. 10] defended the form of federal government proposed by the Constitution. Critics of the Constitution argued that the proposed federal government was too large and would be unresponsive to the people.
>
> In response, Madison explored majority rule v. minority rights in this essay. He countered that it was exactly the great number of factions and diversity that would avoid tyranny. Groups would be forced to negotiate and compromise among themselves, arriving at solutions that would respect the rights of minorities. Further, he argued that the large size of the country would actually make it more difficult for **factions** to gain control over others. "The influence of factious leaders may kindle a flame within their particular States, but will be unable to spread a general conflagration through the other States."
>
> —The Bill of Rights Institute

7. Based on the selection above, select the best definition for "faction."

   A. a controlling majority group in a country

   B. a leader who seeks to change the government

   C. a smaller group that disagrees with a larger group

   D. people who work for the government

8. With which of the following statements would Madison agree regarding majority rule and minority rights?

   A. Liberty should not be limited in order to reduce the number of factions.

   B. Liberty should be limited in order to reduce the number of factions.

   C. Majority rule sometimes means minority rights will suffer.

   D. The government should build consensus on all issues.

Amending the Constitution

The United States is governed according to the rules set forth in the Constitution. The Framers of the document created a way to amend—to change or add to—the Constitution through the passage of amendments. As people immigrated to the United States and the country's population grew, the need for a Constitution that could grow and change with the expanding population was evident.

Directions: Read the following questions. Then select the correct answers.

9. The first four amendments of the Bill of Rights addressed which of the following concerns held by the colonists?

   A. unfair court procedures

   B. discrimination based on race

   C. power held by the states not reserved for the central government

   D. basic rights violated by Britain before the Revolutionary War

10. Which two steps are required in the process of changing, or amending, the Constitution?

    A. proposing an amendment in Congress and ratifying the amendment by a majority of states

    B. passing of the amendment in the House and then passing of the amendment in the Senate

    C. passing of the amendment in Congress and then by a minority of states

    D. ratifying the amendment and agreement by a majority of states

Directions: Use the graph below to answer question 11.

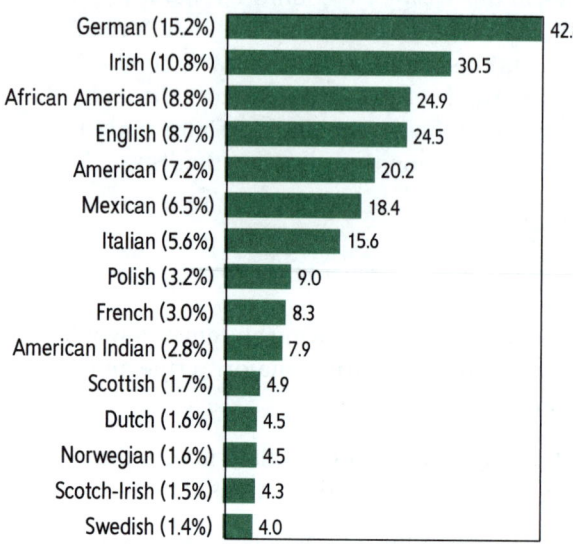

Fifteen Largest Ancestries: 2000
In millions, percentage of total population in parentheses.

- German (15.2%) 42.8
- Irish (10.8%) 30.5
- African American (8.8%) 24.9
- English (8.7%) 24.5
- American (7.2%) 20.2
- Mexican (6.5%) 18.4
- Italian (5.6%) 15.6
- Polish (3.2%) 9.0
- French (3.0%) 8.3
- American Indian (2.8%) 7.9
- Scottish (1.7%) 4.9
- Dutch (1.6%) 4.5
- Norwegian (1.6%) 4.5
- Scotch-Irish (1.5%) 4.3
- Swedish (1.4%) 4.0

Source: U.S. Census Bureau, Census 2000 special tabulation.

11. Asian ancestry is not listed on the bar graph. What can you conclude about its absence from the graph?

   A. Those with Asian ancestry were not large enough to make it to the top fifteen.

   B. The Census Bureau is prejudiced against Asian Americans.

   C. Those of Asian ancestry were combined with another group.

   D. Those with Asian ancestry live mostly in the western United States.

Directions: Read the following question. Then select the correct answer.

12. Because the Constitution can be amended, it will remain _____ throughout time.

   A. legal

   B. relevant

   C. irrelevant

   D. unchanged

✓ Test-Taking Tip

When answering multiple-choice questions, use the process of elimination. First eliminate all answers you know are definitely incorrect. Then analyze the remaining options to determine the correct answer.

Structure of American Government Lesson 1.3

This lesson will help you understand the power of state and federal governments and how both are structured. Use it with core lesson 1.3 Structure of American Government to reinforce and apply your knowledge.

Key Concept
The federal and state governments provide services to people, but they have unique roles and responsibilities.

Core Skills & Practices
- Read a Chart
- Determine Central Ideas

The Three Branches of Government

The Framers of the US Constitution remembered that England's central government had abused its power against the colonists. They were determined to create a new government that had a strong, but limited, central government.

Directions: Read the following questions. Then select the correct answer.

1. Which of the following is the primary job of the president?

    A. to act as commander-in-chief

    B. to sign or veto legislation

    C. to run the executive department

    D. to entertain and inform foreign diplomats

2. Which of the following is not a power of the president?

    A. the power to propose an annual budget

    B. the power to propose legislation

    C. the power to sign treaties

    D. the power to declare war

3. How does the legislative branch exercise its checks and balances toward the executive branch?

    A. It can override a presidential veto.

    B. It can make its own appointments to the Supreme Court.

    C. It can enter into treaties without presidential approval.

    D. It has the power to name ambassadors to foreign nations.

4. Which of the following was the judicial branch's original area of responsibility?

    A. Issues within the legislative branch.

    B. Issues between the executive and legislative branches.

    C. Cases involving leaders of other nations and cases between states.

    D. Cases involving the appointment of judges at a state level.

Directions: Read the passage below. Then answer question 5.

> "I do solemnly swear (or affirm) that I will faithfully execute the office of President of the United States, and will to the best of my ability, preserve, protect and defend the Constitution of the United States." (Oath of Office of the President of the United States)

5. Which part of the oath of office applies to the president's primary job?

   A. "I . . . will faithfully execute the office of president"

   B. "I will . . . preserve . . . the Constitution"

   C. "I will . . . protect . . . the Constitution"

   D. "I will . . . defend . . . the Constitution"

Questions: Use the passage below to complete questions 6 and 7.

> To members of Congress, the president now looms large in the legislative process. He sets the national agenda and has behind him the vast knowledge and expertise of the federal bureaucracy. In this media-driven age, he speaks with one voice, as against the many of Congress, making it easier for him to command the attention of the cameras.
>
> —Radio broadcast of Lee Hamilton, US Representative to Congress from Indiana (1965–1999)

6. Because of the _____, the president in the modern era can speak directly to the people, allowing his _____ to be heard over the voices of Congress.

7. In the past, the _____ had a more direct connection to the people as their representatives.

8. George Washington was the first of several generals who later became president. Think about this statement: A good general makes a good president. Is this an opinion or a fact? Do you agree or disagree with this statement? Explain your responses on a separate sheet of paper.

✓ Test-Taking Tip

During an exam, it often helps to take a momentary break, shut your eyes, and take a few deep breaths. It will help you clear your head and stay fresh during the exam session. Just two or three 30-second breaks can be very beneficial.

The Power of State Government

Besides the central government, the states also hold power. In some cases, they share powers with the central government. Some state powers, however, are held only by the states. The Constitution makes it clear that any powers not named specifically for the federal government are reserved for the states.

Directions: Use the chart below to answer question 9.

9. After each power, write the level of government—federal or state—which holds that power. If it is a power of both levels, then write Federal and State after the power.

Separate and Shared Powers of the Federal and State Governments

Power	
To levy taxes	To hold elections
To enter into treaties with foreign countries	To establish schools
To set up local and county governments	To borrow money
To regulate trade within a state	To declare war

Federal	State	Federal and State

Directions: Use the passage below to answer questions 10 and 11.

McCulloch v. *Maryland* (1819)

In 1816 Congress established the Second National Bank to help control the amount of unregulated currency issued by state banks. Many states questioned the constitutionality of the national bank. Maryland set a precedent by requiring taxes on all banks not chartered by the state. In 1818 the State of Maryland approved legislation to impose taxes on the Second National Bank chartered by Congress.

James W. McCulloch, a federal cashier at the Baltimore branch of the US bank, refused to pay the taxes imposed by the state. Maryland filed a suit against McCulloch in an effort to collect the taxes. The Supreme Court, however, decided that the chartering of a bank was an implied power of the Constitution, under the "elastic clause," which granted Congress the authority to "make all laws which shall be necessary and proper for carrying into execution" the work of the federal government.

... The proceedings posed two questions: Does the Constitution give Congress power to create a bank? And could individual states ban or tax the bank? The court decided that the federal government had the right and power to set up a federal bank and that states did not have the power to tax the federal government. Marshall ruled in favor of the federal government and concluded, "the power to tax involves the power to destroy."

10. The power to set up a bank is shared by both the state and federal government. This is known as a _____ power.

A. equilateral

B. concurrent

C. reserved

D. identical

11. Chief Justice Marshall said "the power to tax involves the power to destroy." Marshall most likely meant that the _____ governments could use that power to weaken the _____ government.

A. federal; state

B. state; judicial

C. federal; local

D. state; federal

The Structure of State Government

The state governments are organized similarly to the central government. They have the same three branches (executive, legislative, and judicial).

Directions: Answer the following questions.

12. The chart below contains the responsibilities of a state governor. Write the role of a governor next to the corresponding responsibility contained in the chart.

Role	Responsibility
	heads his or her political group in the state
	denies or grants paroles, pardons, and reprieves
	sees that state laws are carried out, prepares an annual budget, appoints officials
	proposes, approves, or vetoes legislation
	is head of the National Guard of the state
	represents the state at functions, greets key visitors

| chief executive | party leader | judicial leader |
| ceremonial leader | chief legislator | commander-in-chief |

13. Citizens of a state can exercise three important powers in their state. Which of the following is NOT one of those powers?

A. impeachment

B. direct initiative

C. referendum

D. recall

14. If the governor of a state is equivalent to the president of the US, which of the following offices would be equivalent to the vice president?

A. secretary of state

B. attorney general

C. lieutenant governor

D. state auditor

Individual Rights and Responsibilities Lesson 2.1

This lesson will help you understand how civil rights have progressed for US citizens, particularly for African Americans and women. Use it with core lesson 2.1 Individual Rights and Responsibilities to reinforce and apply your knowledge.

Key Concept
Constitutional amendments and new laws have helped extend civil rights to more people in the United States.

Core Skills & Practices
- Identify Point of View
- Identify Cause-and-Effect Relationships

Civil Rights and Civil Liberties
Freedoms that are guaranteed by the US Constitution are called civil liberties. Civil rights are the rights of full citizenship and equality under the law.

1. Categorize each term as either a civil liberty or a civil right by writing each term in the correct box.

   gathering peacefully   **voting**   **attending school**
   speaking your opinion   **living where you choose**   **employment**

   Civil Liberties   Civil Rights

   [ ]   [ ]

Directions: Read the passage below. Then answer the questions that follow.

> ... in all capital or criminal prosecutions a man has a right to demand the cause and nature of his accusation, to be confronted with the accusers and witnesses, to call for evidence in his favor, and to a speedy trial by an impartial jury ...
>
> —*Virginia Declaration of Rights,* George Mason, 1776

2. George Mason's point of view regarding the rights of the accused is reflected in what Constitutional amendment?

   A. First Amendment

   B. Sixth Amendment

   C. Fourteenth Amendment

   D. Nineteenth Amendment

3. The fact that the authorities cannot search a person's home without a warrant is an example of

   A. double jeopardy.

   B. due process.

   C. the Free Exercise Clause.

   D. the Establishment Clause.

2014 GED® Test Exercise Book

Directions: Read the following excerpt from the Supreme Court's decision in the case of *Miranda* v. *Arizona* (1966). Then answer the question that follows.

> ... the person in custody must, prior to interrogation, be clearly informed that he has the right to remain silent, and that anything he says will be used against him in court; he must be clearly informed that he has the right to consult with a lawyer and to have that lawyer with him during interrogation, and that, if he is indigent, a lawyer will be appointed to represent him.

4. The Warren Court most likely based its decision in *Miranda* v. *Arizona* on what Constitutional amendment?

   A. First Amendment

   B. Fourth Amendment

   C. Fifth Amendment

   D. Fifteenth Amendment

Civil Rights for African Americans

The end of the Civil War eliminated slavery and also extended civil rights to all males born or naturalized in America.

Directions: Read the following questions. Then select the correct answer.

5. Which amendments to the Constitution guaranteed civil rights to newly freed African Americans?

   A. Eleventh, Tenth, Twelfth

   B. Fourteenth, Fifteenth, Sixteenth

   C. Thirteenth, Fourteenth, Fifteenth

   D. Sixteenth, Seventeenth, Eighteenth

6. The Supreme Court ruling in *Plessy* v. *Ferguson* (1896) stated that:

   A. African Americans could not be kept from running for office.

   B. schools for African American children did not have to be built.

   C. segregation was legal as long as facilities were "separate but equal."

   D. African Americans had the equal right to own land.

 Test-Taking Tip

When trying to determine the correct answer to a multiple-choice question, begin by deciding the correct answer before looking at the answer choices. Then, match the answer you believe to be correct with one of the possible choices.

Directions: Read the quote below from Martin Luther King, Jr. Then answer the question that follows.

> Any law that degrades human personality is unjust. All segregation statutes are unjust because segregation distorts the soul and damages the personality. It gives the segregator a false sense of superiority and the segregated a false sense of inferiority.

7. Dr. King's point of view is most clearly reflected in

    A. due process.

    B. *Plessy* v. *Ferguson.*

    C. *Brown* v. *Board of Education, Topeka, Kansas*

    D. the Establishment Clause of the First Amendment.

Women's Rights

After the Civil War, the women who championed voting rights for African American men turned their attention toward securing the same rights for women.

Directions: Read the excerpt below from Sojourner Truth's speech at the Women's Rights Convention in Akron, OH, 1851. Then answer questions 8–9.

> That man over there says that women need to be helped into carriages, and lifted over ditches, and to have the best place everywhere. Nobody ever helps me into carriages, or over mud-puddles, or gives me any best place! And ain't I a woman? Look at me! Look at my arm! I have ploughed and planted, and gathered into barns, and no man could head me! And ain't I a woman? I could work as much and eat as much as a man—when I could get it—and bear the lash as well! And ain't I a woman? I have borne thirteen children, and seen most all sold off to slavery, and when I cried out with my mother's grief, none but Jesus heard me! And ain't I a woman?

8. What is the main idea of Sojourner Truth's speech?

    A. African American men and all women both suffered the same ills.

    B. Women are as able as men.

    C. Women need special rights not given to men.

    D. Enslaved female workers suffered more than enslaved male workers.

9. What does she mean when she says "no man can head me"?

    A. No man could outwork her.

    B. No man could rule over her.

    C. No man could mistreat or abuse her.

    D. No man could be more intelligent than she was.

Directions: Read the following questions. Then select the correct answer.

10. Write the letter in the circle that correctly corresponds to the date on the timeline below. Then circle the events that had a direct effect on improvements in women's rights.

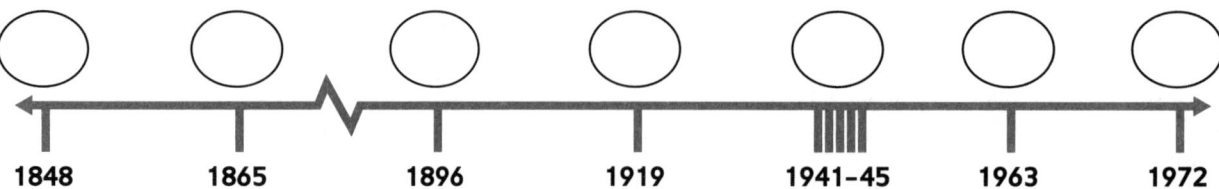

a. passage of the Thirteenth Amendment

b. publication of Betty Friedan's *The Feminine Mystique*

c. Seneca Falls Conference

d. Congress approves the Equal Rights Amendment

e. World War II

f. *Plessy* v. *Ferguson*

g. passage of the Nineteenth Amendment

11. Civil rights for African Americans and for women took a long time and much dedication and hard work before they were granted. Which of the following words *best* describes what it took to achieve this?

A. patience

B. influence

C. suffrage

D. perseverance

12. Title IX guarantees equality for girls and women in which area?

A. medicine

B. sports

C. banking

D. employment

13. James Madison once wrote that "Equal laws, protecting equal rights, are... the best guarantee of loyalty and love of country." On a separate sheet of paper, write a paragraph explaining what you think Madison meant by his statement.

Political Parties, Campaigns, and Elections Lesson 2.2

This lesson will help you understand the role of political parties in US politics, and how interest groups and individuals participate in our democracy. Use it with core lesson 2.2 Political Parties, Campaigns, and Elections to reinforce and apply your knowledge.

Key Concept
People can make their views known and influence public policy through political parties and interest groups.

Core Skills & Practices
- Analyze Ideas
- Interpret Political Cartoons

American Political Parties

Political parties are organizations of like-minded individuals who work to influence national policies by nominating candidates for elected office.

Directions: Read the excerpt below from Senator Barack Obama's speech at the 2004 Democratic National Convention. Then answer the questions that follow.

> [T]here is not a liberal America and a conservative America—there is the United States of America. There is not a black America and a white America and Latino America and Asian America; there's the United States of America. The pundits like to slice-and-dice our country into Red States and Blue States; Red States for Republicans, Blue States for Democrats. But I've got news for them, too. We worship an awesome God in the Blue States, and we don't like federal agents poking around in our libraries in the Red States. . . . There are patriots who opposed the war in Iraq and there are patriots who supported it. We are one people, all of us pledging allegiance to the stars and stripes, all of us defending the United States of America.

1. In this speech, Senator Obama was most likely trying to appeal to what group of voters?

   A. ethnic groups

   B. religious voters

   C. independent voters

   D. veterans groups

2. Senator two tasks did Senator Obama's speech most likely achieve?

   A. expressing a party's beliefs

   B. forming a coalition government

   C. nominating a candidate

   D. raising campaign funds

✓ Test-Taking Tip

The more you practice reading different types of texts of different lengths, the better prepared you will be to read and understand passages presented in reading tests. A good way to practice is to read as much as you can about subjects that interest you. Not only will you become a better reader when taking a test, you will also increase your enjoyment of reading.

Directions: Use the chart below to answer questions 3–5.

Third-Party Presidential Candidates		
Below are some third-party or independent candidates in the twentieth century who received a significant percentage of the vote.		
Candidate	Party	% of vote
Theodore Roosevelt (1912)	Progressive Party	27
Eugene Debs (1912)	Socialist Party	7
Robert M. LaFoliete (1924)	Progressive Party	17
George Wallace (1968)	American Independent Party	14
John B. Anderson (1980)	National Unity Campaign	7
H. Ross Porot (1992)	(Independent)	19
H. Ross Perot (1996)	Reform Party	9
Ralph Nader (2000)	Green Party	3

3. Based on what you have learned about third parties in American politics, what can you conclude about the elections listed in the chart above?

   A. Neither the Democratic nor the Republican Party held a nominating convention in these election years.

   B. Neither the Democratic nor the Republican nominee won enough votes to become president.

   C. Neither the Democratic nor the Republican candidate addressed issues that were important.

   D. Neither the Democratic nor the Republican candidate was able to get enough support to form a coalition government.

4. The elections of 1912, 1980, and 1992 were ones in which the sitting president lost his bid for re-election. Based on this, you can conclude the following:

   A. Third-party candidates can have an effect on the outcome of an election.

   B. The challenger from the opposition party was not able to win a majority of votes.

   C. Most third-party candidates represent extremely radical political views.

   D. Third-party candidates are more powerful now than they were in the past.

5. Why are independents so important to the outcome of modern American elections?

   A. Independents donate more money to political campaigns than members of the major parties.

   B. The numbers of Republicans and Democrats are roughly the same.

   C. The victorious party needs independents to form a coalition government.

   D. The Electoral College is made up mostly of independents.

Political Campaigns and Elections

Political campaigns give voters information about candidates and issues, but the responsibility for investigating, understanding, and making informed decisions resides with each voter.

Directions: Use the political cartoon below to answer questions 6–7.

6. In American politics, an elephant is normally the symbol of the

   A. Electoral College.
   B. Republican Party.
   C. Democratic Party.
   D. House of Representatives.

7. What characteristic(s) allows you to conclude that the image is a political cartoon (as opposed to another kind of artwork)?

   A. The image is a realistic depiction of political events.
   B. The image was drawn by a prominent political figure.
   C. The image combines symbols and caricatures to make a point.
   D. The image is a crudely drawn pencil sketch.

Directions: Use the chart below to answer question 8.

2000 Presidential Election				
Party	Candidate	Electoral Votes	Popular Votes	% of Popular Vote
Republican	George W. Bush	271	50,455,156	47.9
Democrat	Albert Gore, Jr.	266	50,992,335	48.4
Green	Ralph Nader	0	2,882,738	2.7

8. What can you conclude based on the information in this chart?

   A. Without a third-party candidate, George W. Bush would have won the popular vote.

   B. It is possible for a candidate to win the presidency without winning the popular vote.

   C. Of all the candidates, George W. Bush ran the most effective and efficient campaign.

   D. Ralph Nader was a relatively unknown candidate at the time of the election.

The Influence of Interest Groups

Interest groups influence the political process through public advocacy, by campaigning during elections, and by donating money to candidates.

Directions: Read the quote below. Then answer the question that follows.

> . . . we are expected to govern with integrity, good will, clear convictions, and a servant's heart. I pledge to all Americans that I will carry myself in this spirit as vice president of the United States. This was the spirit that brought me to the governor's office, when I took on the old politics as usual in Juneau . . . when I stood up to the special interests, the lobbyists, big oil companies, and the good-ol' boys network.
>
> —Governor Sarah Palin, 2008 Republican National Convention Address

9. Why do you think Governor Palin made a point of mentioning her opposition to lobbyists?

   A. Lobbyists nominate and campaign for candidates for elected office.

   B. Lobbyists often testify at government hearings for or against proposed laws.

   C. Lobbyists represent only Democratic candidates or liberal interest groups.

   D. Lobbyists charge high fees for their services, and often represent wealthy interests.

Contemporary Public Policy Lesson 2.3

This lesson will help define and identify examples of public policy and to describe how public policies are made. Use it with core lesson 2.3 Contemporary Public Policy to reinforce and apply your knowledge.

Key Concept
Actions taken by the government to address concerns of the voting public are known as public policies.

Core Skills & Practices
- Draw Conclusions
- Evaluate Reasoning

What Is Contemporary Public Policy?

The course of action taken to combat problems affecting the public is known as public policy. Because so many issues and problems exist at any given time, thousands of public policies are currently in effect.

Directions: Use the passage to answer questions 1 and 2.

> We the People of the United States, in Order to form a more perfect Union, establish Justice, insure domestic Tranquility, provide for the common defence, promote the general Welfare, and secure the Blessings of Liberty to ourselves and our Posterity, do ordain and establish this Constitution for the United States of America.
>
> —Preamble to the United States Constitution

1. What is the best definition of the word **domestic** as it is used in this passage?

   A. internal
   B. household
   C. supportive
   D. comfortable

2. What is the best definition of the word **Posterity** as it is used in this passage?

   A. other countries
   B. to be prosperous
   C. future generations
   D. states within the Union

Test-Taking Tip

Remember that when answering vocabulary questions, the correct answer is not always the primary dictionary definition. Combine the context clues given to you in the passage with what you know about the author's purpose to help you determine the intended meaning of the word.

3. In the chart below, identify which body would most likely be responsible for the given policy: city government, state government, or national government.

Type of Policy	Type of government
Setting sanitation and waste collection standards	
Defining military eligibility requirements	
Enforcing local noise ordinances	
Defining requirements for obtaining a driver's license	
Adopting education standards and graduation requirements	
Establishing trade practices with foreign countries	

Directions: Use the policy chart below to answer questions 4 and 5.

4. In the public policy log below, fill in the "Type of Policy" section with the best choice from the terms below.

Policy	Type of policy
Seatbelts must be worn by all passengers in a moving vehicle.	
Trucks cannot exceed posted weight limits on public highways.	
All vehicles must pass an emissions test before being issued a license plate.	
License plate renewal fees will be increased by 10% in the new year.	
Drivers are required to carry medical liability coverage through their auto insurance carrier.	

- healthcare policy
- environmental policy
- public safety policy
- transportation policy
- economic policy

5. Which of the following is an opinion based on the information given in this policy log?

   A. People who are safe drivers should not have to wear seatbelts.

   B. Heavy trucks are causing extensive damage to our state's bridges and roadways.

   C. The materials used in making new license plates are more expensive than before.

   D. Drivers without auto insurance drive up the price of insurance for the rest of us.

How National Policy Is Made

Establishing a national policy is essentially a legal and bureaucratic process, but it can also involve participation by concerned citizens, interest groups, and researchers.

Directions: Use the flow chart below to answer questions 6–9.

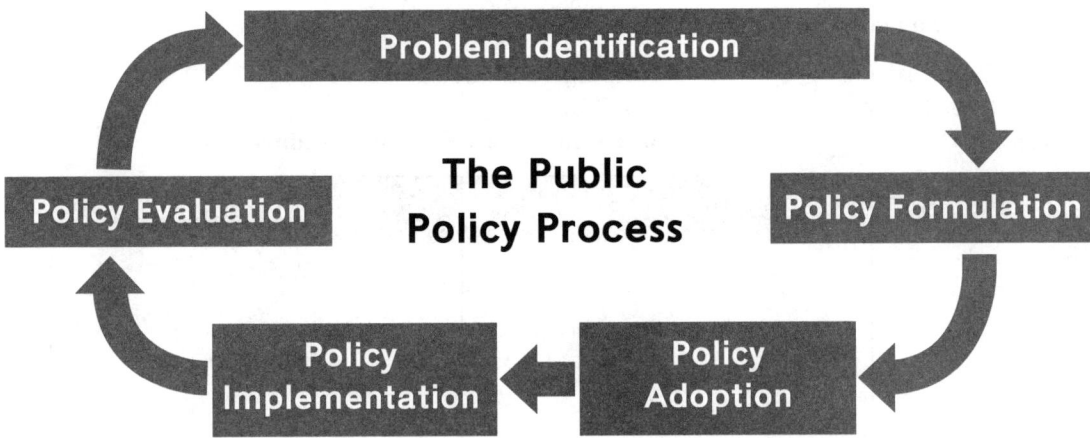

6. Write a number next to the term below to place the steps of the public policy process in the correct order.

   | Policy Implementation | Problem Identification | Policy Adoption |

   | Policy Evaluation | Policy Formulation |

7. What does the shape of this flow chart tell you about the policy-making process?

   A. Any policy solution to one problem will always cause another problem.

   B. Policy-based solutions to problems are never really successful.

   C. Shaping and refining public policy is an ongoing process.

   D. By law, government policies can only last one year and have to be renewed.

8. Suppose the Department of Health and Human Services implemented a policy of providing free flu shots. Which steps would most likely follow in the public policy process?

   A. Health care advocates would work with lawmakers to shape the policy.

   B. Congress would pass a law authorizing the distribution of free flu shots.

   C. Public advocacy groups would identify a sharp rise in the number of flu fatalities.

   D. Medical researchers would examine the benefits of or problems with the program.

9. The _____ step in this process would most likely involve the participation of an interest group?

   A. policy adoption

   B. policy formation

   C. policy evaluation

   D. problem identification

2014 GED® Test Exercise Book

Influences on Public Policy

The government makes public policy, but it is the relationship between the citizens and their government—through voting, interest groups, and lobbyists—that influences which policies are made.

10. Using the table below, categorize each of the following issues as either a special interest group issue, a public interest group issue, or an economic interest group issue.

Relaxing Health Care Regulations
Preventing Texting While Driving
Increasing Voter Registration
Campaign Finance Reform
Gun Control
Improving Work Safety Standards

Special Interest Group	Public Interest Group	Economic Interest Group

Directions: Read the passage below. Then answer questions 11 and 12.

> It is said that lobbying itself is an evil and a danger. We agree that lobbying by personal contact may be an evil and a potential danger to the best in legislative processes. It is said that indirect lobbying by the pressure of public opinion on the Congress is an evil and a danger. That is not an evil; it is a good, the healthy essence of the democratic process.
>
> —US Court of Appeals Ruling in *Rumely* v. *United States*, 1952

11. Which of the following best describes the process of lobbying mentioned in this passage?

A. persuading public officials to adopt particular positions

B. raising awareness about key issues to help voters

C. monitoring public officials to make sure they are not taking bribes

D. electing officials who support policies that help the general public

12. According to this ruling, what type of lobbying practice might be considered "a potential danger to the best in legislative processes"?

A. preparing informational reports for lawmakers

B. giving testimony before Congress

C. hiring a public relations firm to promote an issue

D. personally buying lunch or dinner for government officials

13. Suppose you are the mayor of a city. As mayor, you must address such issues as education, economic growth, crime, preserving the environment, and providing services for the poor. On a separate sheet of paper, write a paragraph identifying which area you would give the highest priority to and explain why.

American Revolution Lesson 3.1

This lesson will help you to understand the causes of the American Revolution, to identify documents that shaped US democratic traditions, to summarize provisions of the Articles of Confederation, and to understand how and why the Constitution was developed. Use it with core lesson 3.1 American Revolution to reinforce and apply your knowledge.

Key Concept

After defeating the British, the new United States established a democratic government built on a foundation of English laws and government.

Core Skills & Practices

- Summarize Ideas
- Analyze Cause and Effect

English Colonies in America

British colonies were established in North America beginning in the late sixteenth century. Colonies in Virginia and New England provided English men and women a place to start a new life. Some sought religious freedom, while others sought economic gain. In each case, the settlements established rules and selected leaders to govern the colonies.

Directions: Use the passage to answer questions 1–4.

> ... having undertaken ... a voyage to plant the first colony in [North America], [we] do ... covenant and combine ourselves together into a civil body politic, for our better ordering and preservation ... and by virtue hereof to enact, constitute and frame such just and equal laws, ordinances, acts, constitutions and offices, from time to time as shall be thought most meet and convenient for the general good of the Colony ...
>
> —The Mayflower Compact

1. What was the purpose of this document?

   A. It authorized Sir Walter Raleigh to set up a colony in North America.

   B. It explained why the Pilgrims broke with the Church of England.

   C. It established the rules by which the Pilgrims would govern themselves.

   D. It gave the Pilgrims large portions of land in Massachusetts.

2. How were the settlers who created this document different from the people who settled in Pennsylvania?

   A. Settlers in Pennsylvania were more tolerant of religious differences.

   B. Pennsylvania did not have a written law code.

   C. The people who settled in Pennsylvania were not from England.

   D. The Pennsylvania colony was not as successful as the Massachusetts colony.

3. This document is an early example of a(n)

   A. boycott.
   B. charter.
   C. constitution.
   D. unicameral.

4. What is the definition of the word **colony** as it is used in this passage?

   A. a voyage of discovery
   B. a religious organization
   C. a land controlled by another nation
   D. a market for another country's goods

The American Revolution

As Britain's empire in America grew, so did the expenses for governing colonies so far away. The costs of providing an army and material goods put a strain on England's economy. Taxes and other policies set forth by the King and Parliament were deemed unfair by many colonists. They felt no one in England was representing their cause before the governing bodies.

Directions: Read the passage below. Then answer the questions that follow.

> Let these *truths* be indelibly impressed on our minds—*that* we *cannot be* HAPPY, *without being* FREE—that we cannot be free, *without being secure in our property*—that *we* cannot be secure in our property, *if, without our consent, others may, as by right, take it away*—that *taxes imposed on us by parliament*, do thus take it away—that *duties laid for the sole purpose of raising money*, are taxes—that *attempts* to lay such duties *should be instantly and firmly opposed*—that this opposition can never be effectual, *unless it is the united effort of these provinces...*
>
> (excerpt from "Letter XII," *Letters from a Farmer in Pennsylvania* by John Dickinson, 1768)

5. Dickinson was most likely writing in opposition to which of the following?

   A. the Townshend Acts
   B. the Boston Massacre
   C. the American Revolution
   D. the Continental Congress

6. The main reason most colonists opposed British taxes was that they

   A. could not raise enough money to pay the taxes.
   B. preferred to pay taxes to the French government.
   C. believed that paying taxes went against their religion.
   D. had no representatives in the British Parliament.

7. Many colonists responded to the taxes mentioned in Dickinson's letter by participating in

   A. colonies.
   B. boycotts.
   C. minutemen.
   D. declarations.

8. What is the definition of the term **indelibly** as it is used in this passage?

   A. hesitantly
   B. temporarily
   C. permanently
   D. without delay

Directions: Read the passage below. Then answer the questions that follow.

> We therefore beseech your Majesty, that your royal authority and influence may be graciously interposed to procure us relief from our afflicting fears and jealousies . . . and to settle peace through every part of our Dominions . . . and that, in the mean time, measures may be taken for preventing the further destruction of the lives of your Majesty's subjects; and that such statutes as more immediately distress any of your Majesty's Colonies, may be repealed.

9. This passage was most likely taken from

   A. the Declaration of Independence.

   B. the Olive Branch Petition.

   C. the Mayflower Compact.

   D. the Articles of Confederation.

10. This document was written in response to

    A. the Boston Massacre.

    B. the Tea Party.

    C. the Stamp Act and the Townshend Acts.

    D. the Battles of Lexington and Concord.

11. King George III responded to this document by

    A. calling for peace.

    B. signing it.

    C. rejecting it.

    D. attacking the colonies.

The Confederation Period

Recognizing the weaknesses of the Articles of Confederation, Congress convened a Constitutional Convention which produced the US Constitution.

Directions: Answer the following questions.

12. In the chart below, identify the characteristics of the Articles of Confederation and the Constitution.

A. Passing laws requires approval of 9 of 13 states	B. Government divided into three branches	C. Representation based on population House of Representatives
D. Each state gets one vote in Senate	E. Congress has no authority to pass taxes	F. Trade regulated by states

Articles of Confederation	Constitution

2014 GED® Test Exercise Book

13. Use the graphic organizer below to place the following events in chronological order from left to right. Second Continental Congress, Constitution Ratified, Stamp Act, Articles of Confederation, Battle of Yorktown, Great Compromise, Boston Massacre, Treaty of Paris, Battles of Lexington and Concord

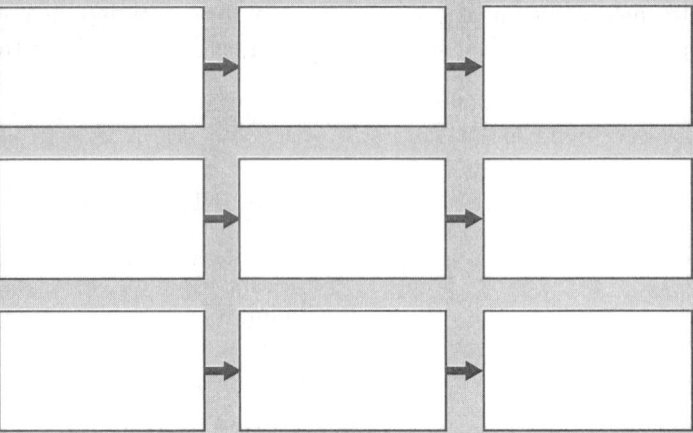

14. On a separate sheet of paper, write an essay in which you compare and contrast the differences and similarities between the ideals of the authors of the Constitution and the status of enslaved people and women in the 1700s.

Test-Taking Tip

You don't always need to remember specific dates to fill in timelines. Just try to focus on what caused specific events. For example, we know that the Second Continental Congress was called for a reason – what was it? Try to link this reason to events that might be related to it.

A New Nation Lesson 3.2

This lesson will help you understand how the United States grew geographically, identify the causes and consequences of the War of 1812, and explain how westward expansion affected Native American policy. Use it with core lesson 3.2 A New Nation to reinforce and apply your knowledge.

Key Concept
After the Revolutionary War, the United States endured conflicts within and struggled with other countries as well.

Core Skills & Practices
- Relate Ideas Within Text
- Sequence Events

The Growth of the Nation

The expansion of the new United States was aided by the Northwest Ordinance of 1787 and the newly ratified Constitution, which created a federal government with a much stronger executive branch than that of the Articles of Confederation and a new president, George Washington.

Directions: Read the passage below. Then answer the questions that follow.

> So soon as there shall be five thousand free male inhabitants of full age in the district, upon giving proof thereof to the governor, they shall receive authority, with time and place, to elect a representative from their counties or townships to represent them in the general assembly . . .

1. This passage is most likely taken from the

   A. United States Constitution.

   B. Articles of Confederation.

   C. Treaty of Paris.

   D. Northwest Ordinance of 1787.

2. This document dealt with the organization of the western lands controlled by the United States; these lands are referred to as _____.

3. _____ states were added to the Union as a result of this document.

Test-Taking Tip

When answering a fill-in-the-blank question, if the blank occurs within a sentence, make sure the sentence makes sense after writing in your answer. Keep track of verb tenses when writing text and use appropriate units when writing numbers.

Directions: Use the chart below to answer questions 4 and 5.

Roles and Responsibilities of the Executive Departments

Department	Leader's Title	Main Area of Responsibility
State Department	Secretary of State	dealing with other nations
Treasury Department	Secretary of the Treasury	looking after the nation's finances
War Department	Secretary of War	defending the nation

4. The offices described in this chart were created by

   A. popular vote.

   B. an act of Congress.

   C. presidential appointment.

   D. an article of the Constitution.

5. Which department would be involved in monitoring conflict between nations that are allies of the United States?

   A. War Department

   B. State Department

   C. Treasury Department

   D. Secretary of the Treasury

6. Using the chart below, write the letter of the condition that caused each of the following treaties in the bin below.

Treaty of Greenville	Treaty of Paris, 1783	Jay's Treaty	Pinckney's Treaty

A. British troops would not withdraw from American forts.

B. Tecumseh, a Shawnee leader, and other tribes attacked white settlers in the Ohio Valley.

C. The Continental Army defeated the British in the American Revolution.

D. Spain was worried about American interference in its territories in North America.

Directions: Read the passage below. Then answer the questions that follow.

> **Louisiana Purchase Treaty (1803)**
>
> Robert Livingston and James Monroe closed on the sweetest real estate deal of the millennium when they signed the Louisiana Purchase Treaty in Paris on April 30, 1803. They were authorized to pay France up to $10 million for the port of New Orleans and the Floridas. When offered the entire territory of Louisiana—an area larger than Great Britain, France, Germany, Italy, Spain and Portugal combined—the American negotiators swiftly agreed to a price of $15 million.
>
> Although President Thomas Jefferson was a strict interpreter of the Constitution who wondered if the U.S. Government was authorized to acquire new territory, he was also a visionary who dreamed of an "empire for liberty" that would stretch across the entire continent. As Napoleon threatened to take back the offer, Jefferson squelched whatever doubts he had and prepared to occupy a land of unimaginable riches.

7. Why would a strict interpretation of the Constitution have prevented Thomas Jefferson from moving forward with the Louisiana Purchase?

   A. It would have kept him from asking Congress to raise taxes to pay for the land.

   B. It would have kept him from acquiring the land because there was no specific provision for acquiring land in the Constitution.

   C. It would have required him to get approval from each of the states before proceeding with this acquisition.

   D. It would have kept him from entering into a treaty with a foreign country.

8. What did Jefferson consider more important than constitutionality in making this decision?

   A. his popularity with the American people

   B. removing all foreign landowners from America

   C. eradicating slavery in the new territory

   D. providing for future growth of the nation

9. The Louisiana Purchase led directly to the

   A. Lewis and Clark Expedition.

   B. Treaty of Greenville.

   C. War of 1812.

   D. Trail of Tears.

The War of 1812

Issues with Great Britain continued for several years after the American Revolution ended, and soon, war again became inevitable.

Directions: Read the following questions. Then select the correct answers.

10. Which of the following was an outcome of the War of 1812?

    A. an upsurge in American nationalism

    B. the signing of Jay's Treaty

    C. increased tensions with Spain

    D. the establishment of a new American navy

11. Congressmen who pushed for war with Great Britain were referred to as _____.

    A. Doves

    B. Jefferson

    C. Federalists

    D. War Hawks

12. General _____ rose to national prominence following his victory at the Battle of New Orleans.

    A. Adams

    B. Jackson

    C. Jefferson

    D. Washington

Manifest Destiny

In the early 1800s, Americans were angry with the British for impressing American sailors and for taking American ships. On June 18, 1812, Congress declared war against Britain. In 1815, the Treaty of Ghent ended the war. Britain and the United States agreed to restore any territories taken during the war.

Directions: Read the passage below. Then answer the questions that follows.

> The whole continent of North America appears to be destined by Divine Providence to be peopled by one *nation*, speaking one language, professing one general system of religious and political principles, and accustomed to one general tenor of social usages and customs. For the common happiness of them all, for their peace and prosperity, I believe it is indispensable that they should be associated in one federal Union.
>
> —John Quincy Adams

13. In this quote, John Quincy Adams is expressing an idea that became known as

    A. the Annexation of Texas.

    B. from sea to shining sea.

    C. the American Revolution.

    D. Manifest Destiny.

14. Which of the following events can be seen as a direct result of the beliefs espoused by Adams?

    A. Jay's Treaty

    B. the War of 1812

    C. the Annexation of Texas

    D. the Battle of Tippecanoe

15. Which of the following was one of the negative consequences of Adams's declaration?

    A. war with Spain

    B. Native American removal

    C. the Battle of New Orleans

    D. the Louisiana Purchase

Civil War and Reconstruction Lesson 3.3

This lesson will help you understand the causes and effects of the Civil War and help you analyze a writer's point of view and use of persuasive language. Use it with core lesson 3.3 Civil War and Reconstruction to reinforce and apply your knowledge.

Key Concept
The Civil War began as an attempt to preserve the Union, but it ended with the abolition of slavery in the United States.

Core Skills & Practices
- Analyze Point of View
- Recognize Persuasive Language

Slavery in the United States

Though slavery was a vital part of the Southern economy, many northerners began the movement to end slavery.

Directions: Use the map below to answer questions 1 and 2.

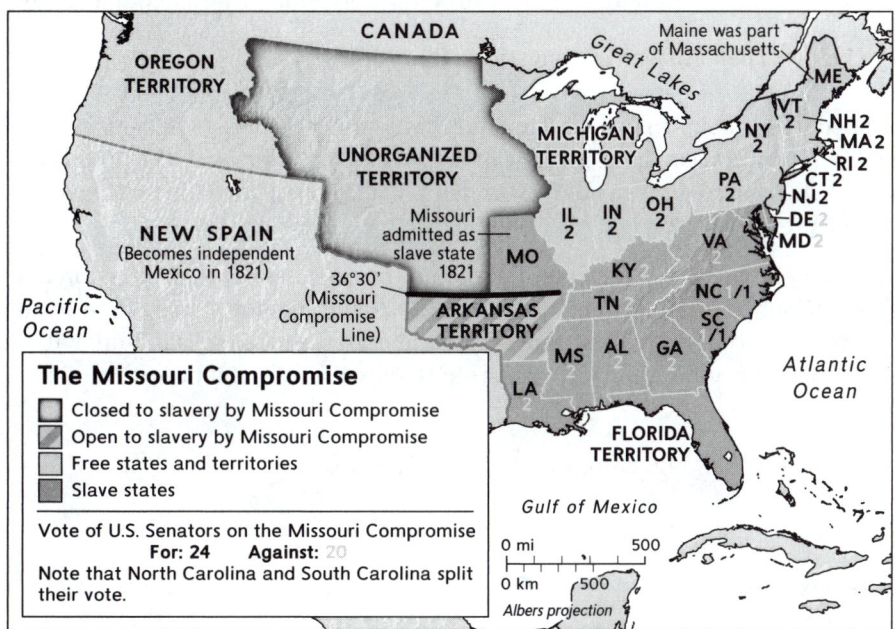

1. Which of the following best explains why it was so important to opponents of slavery that Missouri not enter the Union as a slave state?

   A. Missouri had a higher population of enslaved workers than any other territory.

   B. Most of the country's enslaved workers were purchased in markets in Missouri.

   C. They did not believe that Missouri should have the same rights as the original states.

   D. Its entry would upset the balance between the slave and free states in the Senate.

2. What other state was created as a result of Missouri's admission to the Union?

   A. Michigan

   B. Maine

   C. Louisiana

   D. Oregon

2014 GED® Test Exercise Book

Directions: Read the following questions. Then select the correct answers.

3. People who were opposed to slavery were known as

   A. abolitionists.

   B. slave traders.

   C. confederates.

   D. unionists.

4. Which of the following groups would most likely have supported the expansion of slavery?

   A. poor farmers

   B. factory owners

   C. wealthy planters

   D. newspaper publishers

Civil War

In the spring of 1861, seven southern states seceded from the Union and formed the Confederate States of America. On the morning of April 12, 1861, Confederate guns fired on Fort Sumter and began the Civil War.

Directions: Read the passage below. Then answer the questions that follow.

> In *your* hands, my dissatisfied fellow-countrymen, and not in *mine*, is the momentous issue of civil war. The Government will not assail *you*. You can have no conflict without being yourselves the aggressors. *You* have no oath registered in heaven to destroy the Government, while I shall have the most solemn one to "preserve, protect, and defend it."
>
> I am loath to close. We are not enemies, but friends. We must not be enemies. Though passion may have strained it must not break our bonds of affection. The mystic chords of memory, stretching from every battlefield and patriot grave to every living heart and hearthstone all over this broad land, will yet swell the chorus of the Union, when again touched, as surely they will be, by the better angels of our nature.
>
> —Abraham Lincoln, First Inaugural Address

5. Which of the following best explains why Lincoln stressed that the Union would not provoke a civil war?

   A. Lincoln was not confident in the North's military leadership.

   B. Lincoln did not want to alienate slave states that had stayed in the Union.

   C. Lincoln still thought the Missouri Compromise would settle the issue.

   D. Lincoln knew that the northern economy depended on southern cotton.

6. Lincoln's speech is characterized by his use of

   A. bias.

   B. relevant language.

   C. rhetorical language.

   D. persuasive language.

7. A little more than a month after Lincoln delivered this address, Confederate forces attacked Union troops at

   A. Fort Sumter.

   B. Lexington and Concord.

   C. Gettysburg.

   D. Washington, D.C.

Directions: Use the chart below to answer question 8.

8. Using the terms and the chart below, identify the relative advantages of the North and the South in the Civil War.

| More factories and materials | Familiarity with battlegrounds | More men of military age |

| Only needed to fight to a draw | More railroads and banks | Naval superiority |

North	South

9. On a separate sheet of paper, write a paragraph analyzing how the outcome of the war might have been different if the Confederates had won at Gettysburg.

✓ Test-Taking Tip

When completing a drag-and-drop activity, first check to see which information you recall, and then sort the parts of that known piece of information first. This will shorten the list and make it easier for you to sort the remaining pieces of information, especially if a logical pattern begins to appear.

Reconstruction

The period after the Civil War is known as Reconstruction because it was necessary to restore the Union and fix the destruction in the South caused by the war.

10. Identify the conditions under which former Confederate states were allowed back into the Union by writing the letter for the correct answer choices in the box below.

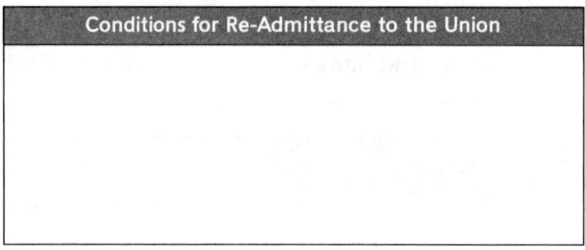

A. The South would be divided into five military districts.

B. States would have to write new constitutions that repealed secession rights.

C. The states would have to ratify the 13th Amendment.

D. Only soldiers below the rank of sergeant would be pardoned.

E. Formerly enslaved people would not be included in any provisions of the plan.

Directions: Read the passage below. Then answer the questions that follow.

> **Section 1.** Neither slavery nor involuntary servitude, except as a punishment for crime whereof the party shall have been duly convicted, shall exist within the United States, or any place subject to their jurisdiction.

11. This excerpt is most likely taken from the

A. Thirteenth Amendment.

B. Fourteenth Amendment.

C. Fifteenth Amendment.

D. Sixteenth Amendment.

12. Many Southern states responded to this amendment by passing

A. slave laws.

B. black codes.

C. the Fourteenth Amendment.

D. indentured servant codes.

13. Northerners originally opposed these measures, but eventually turned away from Reconstruction for reasons that could best be classified as

A. religious.

B. political.

C. economic.

D. ethical.

European Settlement and Population of the Americas Lesson 3.4

This lesson will help you understand why immigrants came to the United States, identify where they settled, and understand how they were received. Use it with core lesson 3.4 European Settlement and Population of the Americas to reinforce and apply your knowledge.

Key Concept
As immigrants came to America, they settled in cities and spread throughout the growing West.

Core Skills & Practices
- Summarize Ideas
- Find Details

The Growth of Immigration

The United States not only grew geographically in the period from 1820 to 1920, but it also grew in population due to the more than 33 million immigrants who moved to the United States from other countries.

Directions: Use the map below to answer questions 1–3.

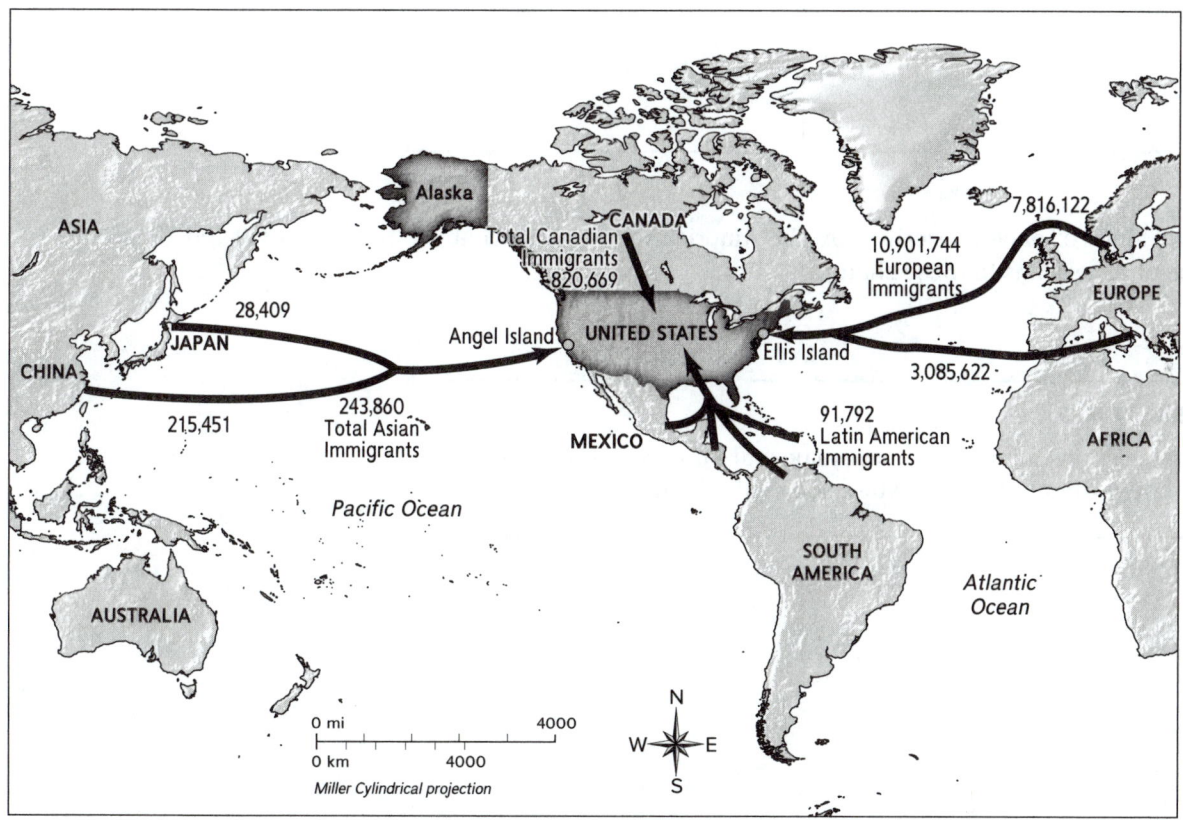

1. Most immigrants from Europe during this period settled in

   A. midwest farms.

   B. east coast cities.

   C. southern plantations.

   D. southwestern ranches.

2. Based on the information in this map, you can conclude that the problem of overcrowding was most pronounced in the

   A. northeast.

   B. west.

   C. midwest.

   D. south.

2014 GED® Test Exercise Book   37

3. The total number of Asian immigrants was _____.

4. Use the terms below to identify the different push factors and pull factors that increase immigration.

| Religious Intolerance | Democracy | Poverty |

| Religious Freedom | Economic Opportunity | Political Oppression |

Push Factors	Pull Factors

5. On a separate sheet of paper, describe how the American population changed between 1820 and 1920 and the response of Americans to these changes.

Test-Taking Tip

When answering questions involving a map, make sure you read the question first so you can know what to look for when you study the map.

Life in America

By the end of the 19th century, more than half of all Americans were living in cities instead of on farms, encouraging a rise of poor living conditions and three distinct social classes.

Directions: Read the passage below. Then answer the questions that follow.

> Be a little careful, please! The hall is dark and you might stumble over the children pitching pennies back there. Not that it would hurt them; kicks and cuffs are their daily diet. They have little else. Here where the hall turns and dives into utter darkness is a step, and another, another. A flight of stairs. You can feel your way, if you cannot see it. Close? Yes! . . . That was a woman filling her pail by the hydrant you just bumped against. The sinks are in the hallway, that all the tenants may have access—and all be poisoned alike by their summer stenches. Hear the pump squeak!... In summer, when a thousand thirsty throats pant for a cooling drink in this block, it is worked in vain. But the saloon, whose open door you passed in the hall, is always there. The smell of it has followed you up. Here is a door. Listen! That short hacking cough, that tiny, helpless wail—what do they mean?
>
> —excerpt from *How the Other Half Lives* by Jacob Riis, 1890

6. The passage is most likely describing life in a

   A. farm.

   B. suburb.

   C. city center.

   D. tenement house.

7. This passage shows that one of the greatest dangers facing immigrants was

   A. gang violence.

   B. poor sanitation.

   C. political corruption.

   D. unsafe working conditions.

8. To combat the problems described in this passage, some reformers created _____, which offered a variety of services that helped poor immigrants.

Directions: Answer the following question.

9. Write the descriptions provided in the table below to accurately describe each social class.

Settled with others of the same ethnic group	Lived in city centers	Lived in neighborhoods on the edge of cities
Commuted to places of work downtown	Owned horses and carriages	Lived farthest from the city center

Social Class Divisions

Upper Class	Middle Class	Lower Class

Discrimination Against Immigrants

Adapting to life in America was not easy for many immigrants, and their differences often made them targets of discrimination.

Directions: Use the chart below to answer questions 10–13.

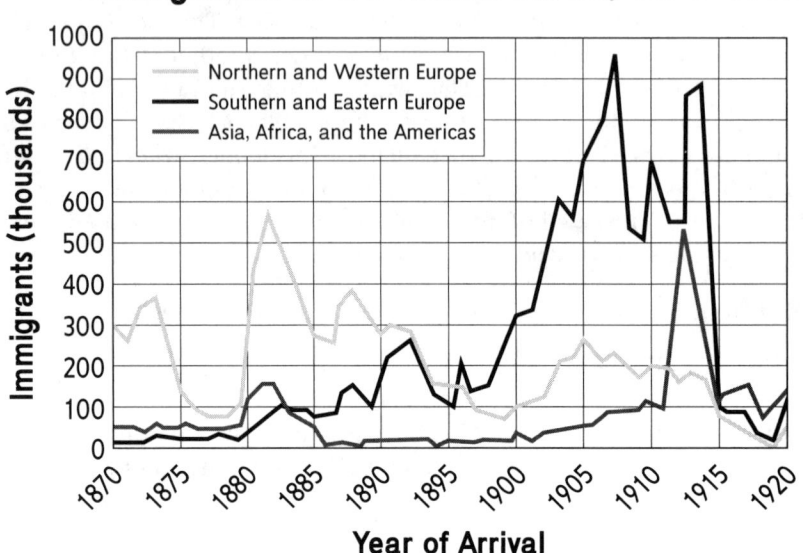

10. Which of the following groups was most opposed to the increase in immigration illustrated in the chart above?

    A. women

    B. Catholics

    C. Progressives

    D. nativists

11. Which of the following best explains why some Americans opposed this new wave of immigration?

    A. Immigrants from southern and eastern Europe had different religions and traditions.

    B. Immigrants tended to push native-born citizens out of the city centers.

    C. Immigrants from Asia and Eastern Europe were opposed to democratic institutions.

    D. Immigrants built new factories that caused pollution and unsafe working conditions.

12. Which of the following best explains the decline in Asian, African, and Latin American immigration between 1880 and 1885?

    A. the Progressive Movement

    B. the Chinese Exclusion Act

    C. the Spanish-American War

    D. the Mexican Revolution

13. In 1885, Northern and Western immigration totaled _____.

World War I Lesson 4.1

This lesson will help you identify the causes of World War I and its effects on Europe and the United States and understand how and why the League of Nations was formed. Use it with core lesson 4.1 World War I to reinforce and apply your knowledge.

Key Concept	Core Skills & Practices
World War I resulted from alliances being formed throughout the world.	• Make Predictions • Sequence Events

The United States Becomes a World Power

By the 1890s, nationalism and imperialism were two sides of the coin that made the United States a nation to be respected before the advent of World War I.

Directions: Read the passage below. Then answer the questions that follow.

> The Spanish-American War grew out of the American public's growing desire to expand American territory and interests and out of a general "war fever."
>
> Several of the larger American newspapers began to capitalize on the Cuban struggle for independence from Spain, sensationalizing abuses the Spanish military forces were committing against the Cubans.
>
> Public outrage reached its peak with the sinking of the battleship [USS] *Maine*, which was sent to the Havana harbor to protect U.S. citizens and property in Cuba. Although the cause of the explosion was never discovered, President McKinley approved a congressional resolution demanding immediate Spanish withdrawal from Cuba. A few days later, Spain declared war.
>
> The congressional resolution stated that the United States was not acting to secure an empire. However, the terms of the Treaty of Paris that officially ended the war required that Spain cede the Philippines, Puerto Rico, and Guam to the United States. For good or ill, the United States had expanded.

1. According to the passage, American involvement in Cuba was most directly triggered by

   A. a desire to help and to protect the less economically fortunate in this world.

   B. a belief that democracy is the only fair form of government.

   C. an overriding desire to maintain peace in the Western Hemisphere.

   D. a sense of outrage about danger to American lives and property abroad.

2. To protect the new US position in the world, Congress allocated money for building

   A. more miles of railroad.

   B. the supply of steel and oil.

   C. a larger navy.

   D. markets for American goods.

World War I

The Great War, later known as World War I, began in Europe in 1914 and a series of alliances brought more and more countries into the conflict, and eventually the United States.

Directions: Read the passage below. Then answer the questions that follow.

> The assassination of Austria-Hungary's Archduke Franz Ferdinand in 1914 provided the spark that caused World War I. The archduke was killed by Gavrilo Princip, a Serbian nationalist. The Serbs supported independence for the Slavs, who lived in Austria-Hungary and wanted recognition as their own independent nation. Very quickly, Austria-Hungary declared war on Serbia.

3. Austria-Hungary's declaration of war against Serbia led to a wider conflict because

   A. Austria-Hungary's actions angered the United States.

   B. Serbia had a large colonial empire.

   C. Serbia was allied with the Allied Powers.

   D. Franz Ferdinand was beloved throughout Europe.

4. Austria-Hungary was involved in a wider _____, or group of countries joined together by a common cause, with Germany and the Ottoman Empire.

   A. alliance

   B. coalition

   C. assembly

   D. union

Directions: Read the passage below. Then answer the questions that follow.

> We intend to begin on the first of February unrestricted submarine warfare. We shall endeavor in spite of this to keep the United States of America neutral. In the event of this not succeeding, we make Mexico a proposal of alliance on the following basis: make war together, make peace together, generous financial support, and an understanding on our part that Mexico is to reconquer the lost territory in Texas, New Mexico, and Arizona.

5. This passage was most likely taken from the

   A. German Alliance.

   B. Hungarian Declaration.

   C. Zimmermann Telegram.

   D. League of Nations Constitution.

6. Which of the following best explains the reason for US neutrality before this document was made public?

   A. The United States was not certain which side would win the war.

   B. Some Americans favored the Allies, but others favored the Central Powers.

   C. Germany had formed an alliance with Mexico, an ally of the United States.

   D. The United States wanted peace but favored Serbian independence.

7. The "unrestricted submarine warfare" described in this passage caused

   A. the destruction of Great Britain's navy.

   B. Russia's withdrawal from the war.

   C. the creation of the Fourteen Points.

   D. Congress's declaration of war on Germany.

Directions: Use the map below to answer questions 8 and 9.

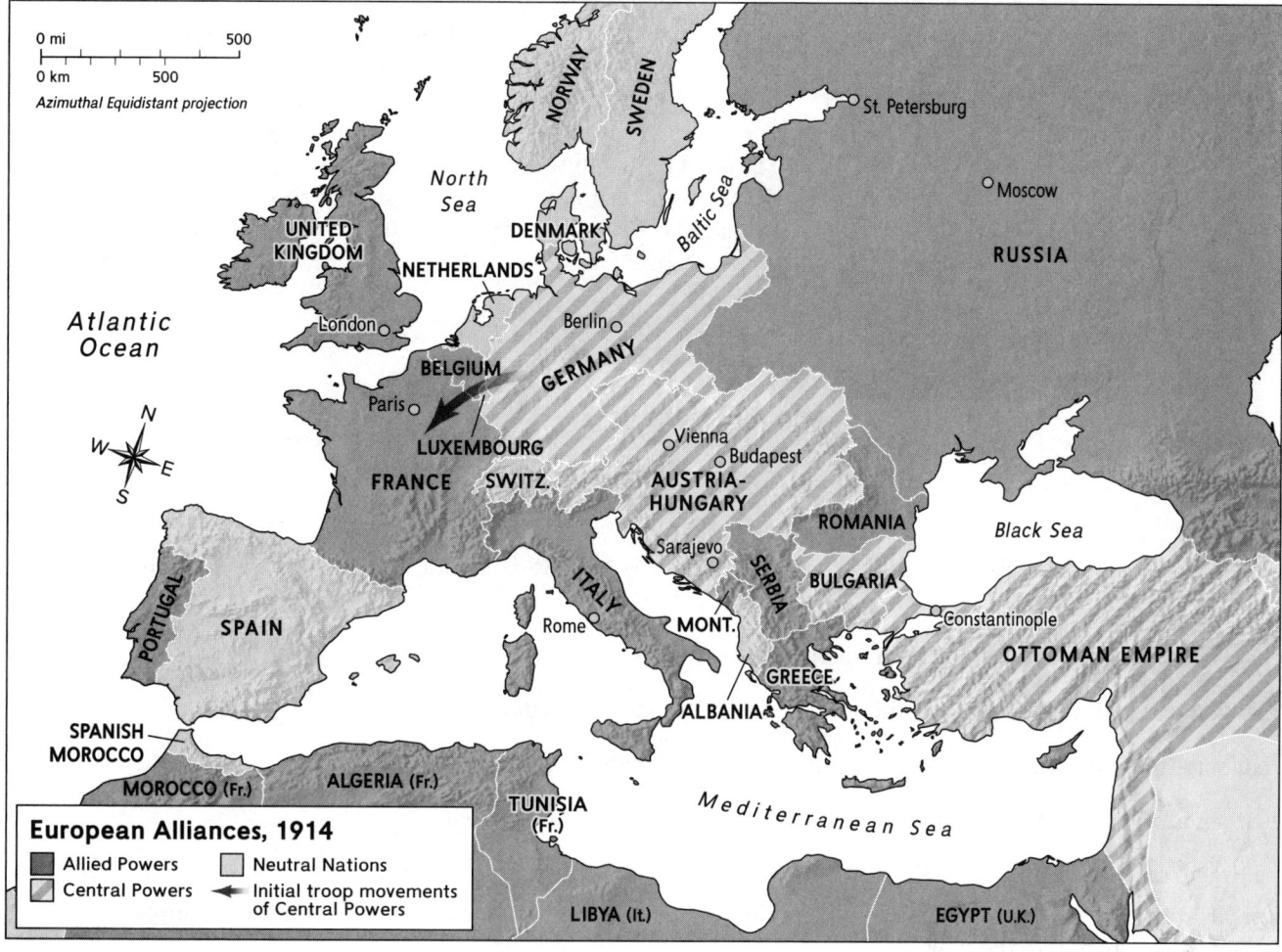

8. One of the biggest disadvantages faced by Germany at the beginning of the war was that it

   A. was surrounded by neutral nations.

   B. had to fight a war on two fronts.

   C. had no access to the Mediterranean Sea.

   D. was separated from its allies.

9. Initial troop movement of the Central Powers began in _____ and moved into France.

   A. Spain

   B. Russia

   C. Germany

   D. Austria-Hungary

10. What was the main result of Russia's withdrawal from World War I?

    A. It gave Germany control of the Black Sea.

    B. It forced Russia to give up control of Serbia and Romania.

    C. It coerced the Allied Powers into negotiating the Treaty of Versailles.

    D. It allowed Germany to focus its forces on the Western front.

Directions: Read the passage below. Then answer the questions that follow.

> We entered this war because violations of right had occurred which touched us to the quick and made the life of our own people impossible unless they were corrected and the world secure once for all against their recurrence. What we demand in this war, therefore, is nothing peculiar to ourselves. It is that the world be made fit and safe to live in; and particularly that it be made safe for every peace-loving nation which, like our own, wishes to live its own life, determine its own institutions, be assured of justice and fair dealing by the other peoples of the world as against force and selfish aggression. All the peoples of the world are in effect partners in this interest, and for our own part we see very clearly that unless justice be done to others it will not be done to us.
>
> —President Woodrow Wilson, January 8, 1918

11. In this address, President Wilson was most likely expressing his support for the creation of the _____.

12. This speech also reflects Wilson's support for the Treaty of Versailles. How did the views of the US Senate differ from those of Wilson?

    A. Most senators were opposed to US involvement in the war.

    B. Most senators felt that the treaty did not do enough to punish Germany.

    C. Most senators were opposed to the League of Nations created by the treaty.

    D. Most senators refused to recognize the new countries created by the treaty.

13. On a separate sheet of paper, identify why Americans' desire for neutrality began to shift and the impact of America's entrance into the war.

Test-Taking Tip

When answering a fill-in-the-blank question, combine your knowledge of the subject with the information given in the sentence to determine the correct answer.

World War II Lesson 4.2

This lesson will help you understand the following: the events that led to World War II, the alliances formed during the war, why the United States entered the war, and how life in the United States was affected by the war. Use it with core lesson 4.2 World War II to reinforce and apply your knowledge.

Key Concept
After World War I, three totalitarian governments formed in Europe and began World War II.

Core Skills & Practices
- Identify Author's Bias
- Understand the Main Idea

The Rise of Dictators

In the years following World War I, totalitarian leaders such as Adolf Hitler and Benito Mussolini were able to seize power by taking advantage of Europe's political and economic instability.

Directions: Use the passage below to answer questions 1 and 2.

> **Excerpt from Adolf Hitler—Speech before the Reichstag January 30, 1937**
>
> Four years ago, when I was entrusted with the Chancellorship and therewith the leadership of the nation, I took upon myself the bitter duty of restoring the honor of a nation which . . . had been forced to live as a pariah . . . The internal order which we created among the German people offered the conditions necessary to reorganize the army and also made it possible for me to throw off those shackles which we felt to be the deepest disgrace ever branded on a people. . . .
>
> I now state here that, in accordance with the restoration of equality of rights, I shall divest the German Railways and the Reichsbank of the forms under which they have hitherto functioned and shall place them absolutely under the sovereign control of the Government of the German Reich.

1. Why was Hitler able to assume control of Germany's railroads and banks?

    A. German citizens had voted to turn the railroads and banks over to the government.

    B. The German Reichstag budgeted the money necessary to buy the railroads and banks.

    C. The Treaty of Versailles authorized Hitler to take control of these industries.

    D. Hitler had suspended the constitution and could pass whatever laws he wanted.

2. Which of the following phrases is an example of bias in Hitler's speech?

    A. "Four years ago, when I was entrusted with the Chancellorship . . ."

    B. "those shackles which we felt to be the deepest disgrace ever branded on a people . . ."

    C. "place them absolutely under the sovereign control of the Government . . ."

    D. "The internal order we created among the German people . . ."

3. Complete the following chart by writing each item in the correct column to indicate which country is best associated with the name or term in the first row.

Josef Stalin   Seized Ethiopia in 1935   National Socialist Party   Took Czechoslovakia in 1939
Communism   Mussolini   Fascism

Germany	Italy	Russia

World War II

Provoked by Hitler's conquest of much of Western Europe and by a direct assault by Japanese forces, the United States entered World War II in 1941.

Directions: Use the passage below to answer questions 4–7.

> Soldiers, Sailors and Airmen of the Allied Expeditionary Force!
>
> You are about to embark upon the Great Crusade, toward which we have striven these many months. . . . the destruction of the German war machine, the elimination of Nazi tyranny over the oppressed peoples of Europe, and security for ourselves in a free world.
>
> Your task will not be an easy one. Your enemy is well trained, well equipped and battle-hardened. . . .
>
> Much has happened since the Nazi triumphs of 1940-41. [Germany has had] great defeats, in open battle . . . Our air offensive has seriously reduced their strength in the air and their capacity to wage war on the ground. Our Home Fronts have given us an overwhelming superiority in weapons and munitions of war . . . The tide has turned! The free men of the world are marching together to Victory!
>
> I have full confidence in your courage . . . We will accept nothing less than full Victory!
>
> Good luck! And let us all beseech the blessing of Almighty God upon this great and noble undertaking.
>
> —General Dwight D. Eisenhower, June 6, 1944

4. Which of the following is one of the "Nazi triumphs" to which Eisenhower refers in his address?

   A. the Battle of Stalingrad

   B. the attack on Pearl Harbor

   C. the conquest of the Balkans

   D. the defeat of Mussolini

5. Based on the information given in this passage, you can conclude that this speech was most likely given immediately before

   A. Operation Berlin

   B. Battle of the Bulge

   C. The Blitz

   D. D-Day

6. What subsequent development proved that the Allies' mission could truly be considered a "Great Crusade"?

A. the discovery of Nazi concentration camps

B. the development of the atomic bomb

C. the removal of Mussolini from power

D. the peace agreements at the Yalta Conference

7. Which of the following sentences shows that Eisenhower was trying to be somewhat unbiased in parts of his speech?

A. "You are about to embark upon the Great Crusade . . ."

B. "Your enemy is well trained, well equipped and battle-hardened."

C. "The free men of the world are marching together to Victory!"

D. "We will accept nothing less than full Victory!"

Directions: Read the passage below. Then answer the questions that follow.

President Franklin D. Roosevelt

Excerpt from Pearl Harbor Address to the Nation, December 8, 1941

The attack yesterday on the Hawaiian islands has caused severe damage to American naval and military forces. I regret to tell you that very many American lives have been lost. In addition, American ships have been reported torpedoed on the high seas between San Francisco and . . .

. . . Japanese forces attacked Hong Kong . . . Guam . . . the Philippine Islands . . . Wake Island . . .

As Commander in Chief of the Army and Navy, I have directed that all measures be taken for our defense. But always will our whole nation remember the character of the onslaught against us.

No matter how long it may take us to overcome this premeditated invasion, the American people in their righteous might will win through to absolute victory. . . .

I ask that the Congress declare that since the unprovoked and dastardly attack by Japan on Sunday, December 7th, 1941, a state of war has existed between the United States and the Japanese empire.

---

8. On what does Roosevelt depend to make his case for declaring war on Japan?

A. He uses strong descriptions and emotionally charged words to persuade Americans to support the war cause.

B. He uses basic, clear facts to educate the public about the dangers that Japan presents to the United States and the world.

C. He relies on his ability to make his opinions sound reasonable and right to get people to support a war declaration.

D. He invokes the values of America to build a case for joining the war.

9. How does the phrase "will win through to absolute victory" foreshadow the American position toward Japan at the end of the war?

A. The United States demanded their unconditional surrender as the only acceptable end to the war with Japan.

B. It alludes to the weaknesses in the Treaty of Versailles at the end of World War I.

C. Roosevelt was concerned about how negotiations with the Axis Powers would leave doors open for another war.

D. The president wanted to show the world that the United States was not weak and would never negotiate with enemies.

✓ Test-Taking Tip

When answering passage-based questions, it is sometimes a good idea to skim the passage first just to get an idea of the author's general purpose and tone. Then read the questions to guide you through a closer reading of the passage.

Directions: Use the chart below to answer the following question.

10. Complete this chart of the events of 1945 by adding the letter of the correct effect from the list below.

Events of 1945

Cause	Effect
Allied troops surround Germany and head toward Berlin.	
President Roosevelt dies unexpectedly.	
The Germans surrender.	
Japan refuses to surrender unconditionally.	
A second bomb is dropped on Nagasaki.	

Effects

A. An atomic bomb is dropped on Hiroshima.

B. Harry S. Truman is sworn in as president.

C. Hitler commits suicide.

D. The Japanese surrender, and World War II is over.

E. The Allies declare May 8 as V-E Day, for "Victory in Europe."

Americans during the War

On the home front, Americans were unified in their support of the war effort, though many loyal Americans still faced racial and ethnic discrimination.

Directions: Read the passage below. Then answer the questions that follow.

> Now ... as President of the United States, and Commander ... I hereby authorize and direct the [creation of] ... military areas ... from which any or all persons may be excluded, and with respect to which, the right of any person to enter, remain in, or leave shall be subject to ... restrictions ...
>
> —President Franklin D. Roosevelt, United States Executive Order 9066

11. This executive order was mainly targeted at

   A. African Americans.

   B. Jewish Americans.

   C. Latin Americans.

   D. Japanese Americans.

12. As a result of this executive order, many Americans were

   A. drafted into the armed forces.

   B. sent to internment camps.

   C. forced to ration supplies.

   D. moved into urban areas.

The Cold War Lesson 4.3

This lesson will help you understand how communism spread throughout the world, how the United States matured as a world power, and how the world reacted to the Cold War. Use it with core lesson 4.3 The Cold War to reinforce and apply your knowledge.

Key Concept
After World War II, the United States and the Soviet Union began a Cold War that kept tensions high between the countries.

Core Skills & Practices
- Identify Implications
- Use Maps, Charts, and Graphs

A Broken Alliance
Following World War II, the United States and the Soviet Union emerged as the world's superpowers, with competing economic and political philosophies.

Directions: Use the map below to answer questions 1–4.

Europe After World War II
- Communist control
- Divided nation
- NATO member
- Neutral nation
- Jointly-occupied city

1. Based on the map, how was Germany different after World War II?

   A. Germany expanded considerably, gaining new territories from the former Austria-Hungary and from France.

   B. Germany was divided into zones to be occupied by each of the Allied nations, including an eastern zone that became communist.

   C. All of Germany was controlled by the Soviet Union and cut off from the rest of Europe.

   D. Germany was cut up into several smaller nations, each one establishing its own government.

2. On the map, which color represents the countries behind the "iron curtain"?

   A. light gray

   B. medium gray

   C. both dark and light gray

   D. dark gray

3. Why would Berlin as a jointly occupied city be problematic for the western block of nations?

   A. Berlin was deep in the communist-controlled area of Germany and could be vulnerable to Soviet tactics.

   B. Berlin's people would be confused about their government and their future.

   C. Having Berlin divided into two separate zones created a false sense of calm in the region.

   D. The western block of nations had few concerns about Berlin.

4. Based on the map, how might Denmark's role as a UN member be critical to the people of West Germany?

   A. Denmark's economy depended on goods coming from West Germany.

   B. The West Germans could count on the Nordic nations of Denmark, Norway, and Sweden for military support.

   C. The United Nations could depend on Denmark.

   D. The North Sea is West Germany's only outlet to the Atlantic Ocean, and Denmark would be favorable to their incoming or outgoing shipping.

Test-Taking Tip

When answering questions involving historic maps, be sure to incorporate your knowledge of the era in question.

The West Responds to Communism

Fearing the spread of communism following the partition of Germany after World War II, the United States tried to limit the extension of Soviet influence in Europe.

Directions: Read the passage below. Then answer the questions that follow.

> Soviet power, unlike that of Hitlerite Germany, . . . It does not work by fixed plans. It does not take unnecessary risks. Impervious to logic of reason, and it is highly sensitive to logic of force. For this reason it can easily withdraw—and usually does—when strong resistance is encountered at any point. Thus, if the adversary has sufficient force and makes clear his readiness to use it, he rarely has to do so. If situations are properly handled there need be no prestige-engaging showdowns . . .
>
> We must formulate and put forward for other nations a much more positive and constructive picture of [the] sort of world we would like to see than we have put forward in [the] past. It is not enough to urge people to develop political processes similar to our own. Many foreign peoples, in Europe at least, are tired and frightened by experiences of [the] past, and are less interested in abstract freedom than in security. They are seeking guidance rather than responsibilities. We should be better able than Russians to give them this. And, unless we do, Russians certainly will.
>
> —American Diplomat George F. Kennan, 1946

5. The first paragraph expresses a policy toward communism that would later be known as

   A. détente.

   B. democracy.

   C. containment.

   D. foreign aid.

6. Which showed how Truman was able to put the second part of Kennan's analysis into action?

   A. the Yalta Conference

   B. the Marshall Plan

   C. the Bay of Pigs Invasion

   D. the Cuban missile crisis

8. Which international organization carried out Kennan's ideas?

   A. the North Atlantic Treaty Organization

   B. the Warsaw Pact

   C. the United Nations Security Council

   D. the Yalta Conference

7. Using the chart and the actions below, identify the ways that Presidents Truman and Kennedy were able to put Kennan's ideas into action during an international crisis.

| sent troops to West Berlin | airlifted supplies into Berlin | increased defense spending | built bomb shelters across the United States |

International Crises		
Truman	Berlin Blockade	
Kennedy	East German Crisis	

2014 GED® Test Exercise Book

Communism Outside of Europe

As the inauguration of President John Kennedy signaled a new era in American politics, the United States faced new threats in the form of communist governments in Cuba and in Southeast Asia.

Directions: Read the passage below. Then answer the questions that follow.

> To those peoples in the huts and villages of half the globe struggling to break the bonds of mass misery, we pledge our best efforts to help them help themselves, for whatever period is required—not because the communists may be doing it, not because we seek their votes, but because it is right. If a free society cannot help the many who are poor, it cannot save the few who are rich.
>
> To our sister republics south of our border, we offer a special pledge—to convert our good words into good deeds—in a new alliance for progress—to assist free men and free governments in casting off the chains of poverty. But this peaceful revolution of hope cannot become the prey of hostile powers. Let all our neighbors know that we shall join with them to oppose aggression or subversion anywhere in the Americas. And let every other power know that this Hemisphere intends to remain the master of its own house.
>
> —President John F. Kennedy, Inaugural Address

9. One reason Kennedy might have been especially concerned about the plight of "our sister republics south of the border" was that thousands of _____ were fleeing to the United States to escape communism.

10. Critics could argue that he failed to "oppose aggression" in the Americas by refusing to

    A. send spy planes over Cuba.

    B. remove missile sites from the Turkish-Russian border.

    C. allocate money to build bomb shelters in the United States.

    D. provide air cover for the Bay of Pigs invasion.

11. President Johnson carried on the foreign policy outlined in Kennedy's inaugural address by

    A. granting independence to India and Pakistan.

    B. opposing colonial rule in Africa.

    C. increasing the number of troops in Vietnam.

    D. holding peace talks with Nikita Khrushchev.

12. On a separate sheet of paper, explain if you think the conflict in Vietnam was avoidable. Could Kennedy or Johnson have done anything differently to either prevent or win the war in Vietnam? Support your response with facts.

Societal Changes Lesson 4.4

This lesson will help you understand the achievements and failures of the Johnson and Nixon administrations and their connections to the collapse of communism. Use it with core lesson 4.4 Societal Changes to reinforce and apply your knowledge.

Key Concept
During the second half of the twentieth century, the United States struggled with scandals at home and communism abroad.

Core Skills & Practices
- Integrate Concepts Presented in Different Ways
- Paraphrase Information

The Great Society
The presidency of Lyndon Johnson was defined by Great Society programs and the Vietnam War.

Directions: Read the passage below. Then answer the questions that follow.

> The Great Society . . . demands an end to poverty and racial injustice . . . But that is just the beginning. The Great Society is a place where every child can find knowledge to enrich his mind and to enlarge his talents. It is a place where leisure is a welcome chance to build and reflect, not a feared cause of boredom and restlessness. It is a place where the city of man serves not only the needs of the body and the demands of commerce but the desire for beauty and the hunger for community. It is a place where man can renew contact with nature. It is a place which honors creation for its own sake and for what it adds to the understanding of the race. It is a place where men are more concerned with the quality of their goals than the quantity of their goods. But most of all, the Great Society is not a safe harbor, a resting place, a final objective, a finished work. It is a challenge constantly renewed, beckoning us toward a destiny where the meaning of our lives matches the marvelous products of our labor.
>
> —President Lyndon B. Johnson, Great Society Speech, 1964

1. According to the passage, which of these is one major focus of the Great Society?

   A. greater production of goods

   B. increased industrial production

   C. environmental enrichment

   D. greater retirement options

2. If Great Society programs were entirely successful, what would be one likely result?

   A. People of all races would be assured equal rights.

   B. All adult citizens would have more leisure time.

   C. Laws would prevent any adverse effects on the environment.

   D. All citizens could buy the products they wanted.

The Nixon Administration

President Richard Nixon ended the Vietnam War and introduced policies of New Federalism but was eventually forced to resign as a result of the Watergate scandal.

Directions: Read the passage below. Then select the option that correctly completes each sentence.

3. Richard Nixon was the [1 Select...▼] nominee who won the presidency in [2 Select...▼]. In 1973, Nixon participated in the [3 Select...▼], which ended the [4 Select...▼].

   [1 Select...▼]
   A. Democratic
   B. Republican
   C. third party
   D. Independent

   [3 Select...▼]
   A. Vietnam War
   B. Great Society
   C. Voting Rights Act
   D. Paris Peace Accord

   [2 Select...▼]
   A. 1967
   B. 1968
   C. 1972
   D. 1976

   [4 Select...▼]
   A. Vietnam War
   B. Great Society
   C. Voting Rights Act
   D. Paris Peace Accord

4. President Nixon announced his visit to China after what preceding event?

   A. a halt to the Vietnam War
   B. secret negotiations with China's leaders
   C. a treaty with the Soviet Union
   D. agreement to end relations with Taiwan

5. President Nixon visited both China and the Soviet Union in what year?

   A. 1969
   B. 1970
   C. 1971
   D. 1972

Directions: Read the passage below. Then answer the questions that follow.

> Since March, when I first learned that the Watergate affair might in fact be far more serious than I had been led to believe, it has claimed far too much of my time and my attention. Whatever may now transpire in the case, whatever the actions of the grand jury, whatever the outcome of any eventual trials, I must now turn my full attention—and I shall do so—once again to the larger duties of this office. I owe it to this great office that I hold, and I owe it to you—to my country . . . Tomorrow, for example, Chancellor Brandt of West Germany will visit the White House for talks that are a vital element of "The Year of Europe," as 1973 has been called. We are already preparing for the next Soviet-American summit meeting later this year.
>
> This is also a year in which we are seeking to negotiate a mutual and balanced reduction of armed forces in Europe, which will reduce our defense budget and allow us to have funds for other purposes at home so desperately needed. It is the year when the United States and Soviet negotiators will seek to work out the second and even more important round of our talks on limiting nuclear arms and of reducing the danger of a nuclear war that would destroy civilization as we know it. It is a year in which we confront the difficult tasks of maintaining peace in Southeast Asia and in the potentially explosive Middle East.
>
> —President Richard M. Nixon, First Watergate Speech, 1973

6. The Watergate affair that Nixon refers to was a _____ that eventually forced him to resign from office.

   A. scandal

   B. détente

   C. public policy

   D. campaign strategy

7. At the time Nixon gave this speech, which of the following appears to be true?

   A. The House Judiciary Committee had voted for Nixon's impeachment.

   B. Transcripts of White House tapes had been provided to the Congress.

   C. Five men who had broken into Democratic offices had been arrested.

   D. Nixon had decided to resign from the presidency.

8. According to the speech, Nixon was focused on which of these instead of the Watergate affair?

   A. ending communism in the Soviet Union

   B. reducing taxes for working families

   C. increasing American military presence overseas

   D. reducing the worldwide nuclear threat

Test-Taking Tip

When test questions are preceded by a written passage, read the questions first and then look for the answers as you read the passage.

Communism in China and the Soviet Union

Improvements in relations between the United States and communist countries and societal changes over many decades eventually led to the birth of democracy in Eastern European nations and the dissolution of the Soviet Union.

Directions: Read the following questions. The select the correct answers.

9. Which event was a turning point in US relations with China?

   A. President Nixon's visit to China

   B. the fall of the Berlin Wall

   C. the Watergate scandal

   D. the election of Mikhail Gorbachev

10. President Nixon adopted the policy of _____ to relax tensions between the United States and communist countries such as China and the Soviet Union.

    A. detente

    B. containment

    C. public policy

    D. diplomatic silence

11. Nixon's visit to China started diplomatic communications that had previously been cut off during which decade?

    A. 1930s

    B. 1940s

    C. 1950s

    D. 1960s

12. Which of the following events would immediately follow the fall of the Berlin Wall?

    A. democratic elections in Eastern European countries

    B. signing of the Strategic Arms Limitation Treaty

    C. the beginning of a rivalry between China and the USSR

    D. the People's Republic of China joins the United Nations

Foreign Policy in the 21st Century Lesson 4.5

This lesson will help you understand how US government policies changed after the terrorist attacks on September 11, 2001. Use it with core lesson 4.5 Foreign Policy in the 21st Century to reinforce and apply your knowledge.

Key Concept
In the first decade of the twenty-first century, the United States experienced a terrorist attack that reshaped government and policies.

Core Skills & Practices
- Conduct Research Projects
- Evaluate Evidence

Terrorism in the United States
Terrorist attacks on the United States in the 1990s and 2001 were linked to Osama bin Laden and the Middle Eastern terrorist group known as al-Qaeda.

Directions: Use the timeline below to answer questions 1 and 2.

Events Related to Terrorist Attacks on the United States

A. Bombing of American embassies in Kenya and Tanzania

B. Bombing of USS *Cole* in Yemen

C. Planes attack World Trade Center and Pentagon

D. Truck bomb at World Trade Center

E. American troops stationed in Saudi Arabia (Gulf War)

1. Write the letter of each event next to the correct spot on the timeline.

2. Which of the following events would come next after the events on the timeline above?

    A. Osama bin Laden assassinated

    B. weapons of mass destruction found in Iraq

    C. Taliban government overthrown in Afghanistan

    D. Saddam Hussein convicted of crimes against humanity

Directions: Use the passage to answer questions 3 and 4.

> Today, our fellow citizens, our way of life, our very freedom came under attack in a series of deliberate and deadly terrorist acts. The victims were in airplanes or in their offices: secretaries, businessmen and women, military and federal workers, moms and dads, friends and neighbors. Thousands of lives were suddenly ended by evil, despicable acts of terror. The pictures of airplanes flying into buildings, fires burning, huge structures collapsing have filled us with disbelief, terrible sadness, and a quiet, unyielding anger. These acts of mass murder were intended to frighten our nation into chaos and retreat. But they have failed; our country is strong.
>
> A great people has been moved to defend a great nation. Terrorist attacks can shake the foundations of our biggest buildings, but they cannot touch the foundation of America. These acts shattered steel, but they cannot dent the steel of American resolve. America was targeted for attack because we're the brightest beacon for freedom and opportunity in the world. And no one will keep that light from shining. Today, our nation saw evil, the very worst of human nature. And we responded with the best of America—with the daring of our rescue workers, with the caring for strangers and neighbors who came to give blood and help in any way they could.
>
> —President George W. Bush, Address to the Nation, September 11, 2001

3. What does President Bush suggest was a main target of the attacks on September 11, 2001?

    A. American technology

    B. American political views

    C. American commerce

    D. American social values

4. According to Bush, the attack on September 11, 2001, was a **terrorist** attack. This type of attack is characterized by which of these strategies?

    A. use of propaganda to incite violence

    B. use of force to overthrow governments

    C. use of violence to frighten opponents

    D. use of demonstrations to protest policies

Directions: Read the following questions. Then select the correct answers.

5. On September 11, 2001, three of the four hijacked planes reached the hijackers' targets. Where did the fourth plane crash due to its passengers' resistance?

    A. Maryland

    B. Connecticut

    C. Pennsylvania

    D. West Virginia

6. The September 11, 2001 terrorist attacks led to the creation of what federal government agency?

    A. Department of Antiterrorism

    B. Department of Transportation

    C. Federal Aviation Administration

    D. Department of Homeland Security

The Global War on Terror

In response to the terrorist attacks of 9/11, the United States launched an anti-terrorism campaign that has become known as the global war on terror.

Directions: Use the timeline below to answer questions 7 and 8.

Events Related to the War on Terror

A. All American troops removed from Iraq

B. NATO troops invade Afghanistan

C. Osama bin Laden killed in Pakistan

D. American and British troops invade Iraq

E. American embassy established in Baghdad

7. Write the letter of each event next to the correct spot on the timeline.

8. This timeline illustrates the effect that the terrorist attacks of 9/11 had on the United States' _____, or its interactions with other nations.

   A. foreign policy

   B. domestic policy

   C. public policy

   D. foreign aid

 Test-Taking Tip

In order to accurately fill in a timeline, consider which events had to happen before others could occur.

2014 GED® Test Exercise Book

Directions: Read the passage. Then answer questions 9–12.

> (1) North Korea is a regime arming with missiles and weapons of mass destruction, while starving its citizens. (2) Iran aggressively pursues these weapons and exports terror, while an unelected few repress the Iranian people's hope for freedom. (3) Iraq continues to flaunt its hostility toward America and to support terror. (4) The Iraqi regime has plotted to develop anthrax and nerve gas and nuclear weapons for over a decade. (5) This is a regime that has already used poison gas to murder thousands of its own citizens, leaving the bodies of mothers huddled over their dead children. (6) This is a regime that agreed to international inspections then kicked out the inspectors. (7) This is a regime that has something to hide from the civilized world. (8) States like these, and their terrorist allies, constitute an axis of evil, arming to threaten the peace of the world. (9) By seeking weapons of mass destruction, these regimes pose a grave and growing danger. (10) They could provide these arms to terrorists, giving them the means to match their hatred. (11) They could attack our allies or attempt to blackmail the United States. (12) In any of these cases, the price of indifference would be catastrophic.
>
> —President George W. Bush, State of the Union Address, 2002

9. President Bush most likely gave this speech to justify

A. the passage of the Patriot Act.

B. the creation of the Department of Homeland Security.

C. the invasion of Iraq.

D. the assassination of Osama bin Laden.

10. Which of the following sentences includes language that is meant to evoke an emotional response in those hearing the speech?

A. Sentence 3

B. Sentence 5

C. Sentence 7

D. Sentence 9

11. Which of the following sentences about Iraq includes an unsupported claim that cannot be verified by fact-checking?

A. Sentence 4

B. Sentence 5

C. Sentence 6

D. Sentence 7

12. The term "axis of evil" was likely used to accomplish which of these goals?

A. to convince Iran, Iraq, and North Korea to reduce stocks of weapons

B. to provide factual evidence that these countries are dangerous

C. to identify countries that were involved in the 9/11 terrorist attacks

D. to recruit allies to support the United States in any actions against these countries

Markets, Competition, and Monopolies   Lesson 5.1

This lesson will help you understand the nature of markets and how competition and monopolies affect the economy. Use it with core lesson 5.1 Markets, Competition, and Monopolies to reinforce and apply your knowledge.

Key Concept	Core Skills & Practices
Buyers and sellers exchange goods and services in a market. Monopoly occurs when a business in a market has no competition, but with many businesses in a market, competition can thrive.	• Predict Outcomes • Synthesize Ideas from Multiple Sources

Markets

The economy is made of markets in which people and businesses exchange goods and services.

Directions: Read the following questions. Then select the correct answer.

1. Which of the following would be considered a market?

   A. a private golf course

   B. a state forest preserve

   C. a classroom

   D. an aircraft carrier

2. Why did money begin to take the place of barter in market exchanges?

   A. Money made the exchanges more fair.

   B. Money made the exchanges more enjoyable.

   C. Barter was not possible in market exchanges.

   D. Money made the exchanges easier.

3. Sometimes goods and services are provided by the same supplier in the same transaction. For example, an auto repair shop may list the parts (goods) and labor (service) separately. Write each item in the correct bin.

dry cleaning	milk	mowing the lawn
city water	washing machine	a decorated cake

Goods	Services	Goods and Services

Competition

When there is competition in the market, buyers have more choices and more control over how much they have to pay for the goods and services they buy.

Directions: Read the following questions. Then select the correct answers.

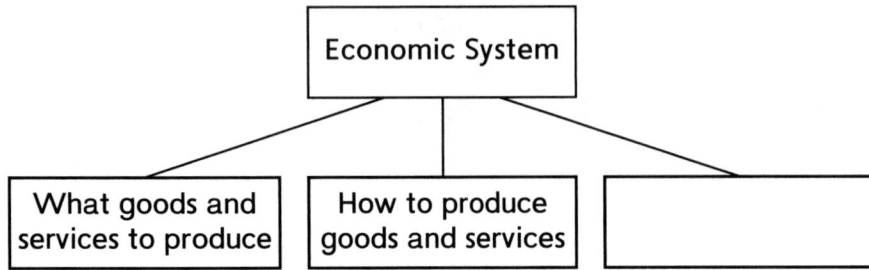

4. Look at the above diagram. Which of the following statements would fit in the third box?

   A. Why to produce them

   B. How much to sell them for

   C. Where to get the resources

   D. For whom to produce them

5. In a market economy, the problem of distribution is largely resolved by _____

   A. price.

   B. government.

   C. wages.

   D. capitalism.

Directions: Read the following advertisement that appeared in a small-town newspaper, and answer the question that follows.

> Ben and Sue's Restaurant, in business for 30 years, features all original recipes from Chef Janison; NOW we are hosting live entertainment every Thurs. through Sat. nights; all local musicians. Come and enjoy the atmosphere; and bring a few friends.

6. The ad is an example of how a business can engage in

   A. specialization.

   B. psychological advertising.

   C. nonprice competition.

   D. service.

 Test-Taking Tip

The more you practice reading different types of texts of different lengths, the better prepared you will be to read and understand passages presented in reading tests. A good way to practice is to read as much as you can about subjects that interest you. Not only will you become a better reader when taking a test, you will also increase your enjoyment of reading.

Directions: Read the passage below. Then answer the questions that follow.

> It is not from the benevolence of the butcher, the brewer, or the baker that we expect our dinner, but from their regard to their own interest. We address ourselves, not to their humanity but to their self-love. . . . Give me what I want, and you shall have this which you want, is the meaning of every such offer; and it is the manner that we obtain from one another the far greater part of those good offices which we stand in need of.
>
> —Adam Smith *The Wealth of Nations*, 1776

7. According to Smith, what roles do benevolence and self-interest have in a transaction?

   A. Both buyers and sellers are motivated by self-interest.

   B. Buyers are motivated by benevolence and not self-interest.

   C. Sellers are motivated by benevolence more than self-interest.

   D. Sellers are motivated by both self-interest and benevolence.

8. If we need meat for dinner, but cannot afford to pay for it, why is it futile to depend on the butcher to provide it for free?

   A. The butcher is not motivated by benevolence.

   B. The butcher wants to be benevolent but can't afford to be.

   C. The butcher must compete with the brewer and the baker.

   D. The butcher is interested only in self-interest.

Directions: Read the questions. Then select the correct answers.

9. In a market economy, who or what forces sellers to respond to consumer needs?

   A. monopoly

   B. government officials

   C. competition

   D. suppliers

10. On a separate sheet of paper, explain the importance of the six conditions for market competitiveness and how each plays a role in the market.

Monopolies

The government has enacted several laws to prevent monopolies from forming.

Directions: Read the passage below. Then answer the question that follows.

> There are several kinds of monopolies. Companies often spend large amounts of money in research to develop new products for which they can acquire patents. This gives them the exclusive right to sell the product for many years.

11. A patent is to a new product, as a _____ is to a work of art.

A. market

B. competition

C. monopoly

D. copyright

Direction: Read the following questions. Then select the correct answer.

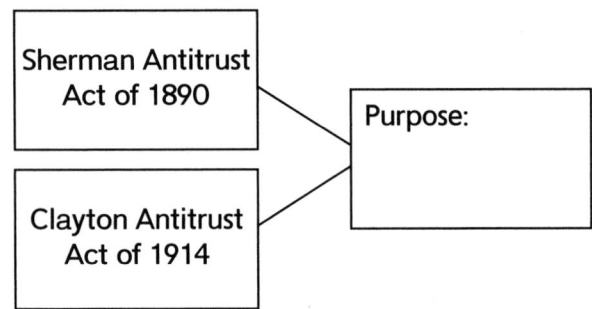

12. Look at the diagram above. What was the purpose of these two acts?

A. to prevent monopolies

B. to encourage research and development

C. to protect patents

D. to interfere with markets

13. Which of these market characteristics pertain to a monopoly?

A. Many buyers and sellers in the market each account for only a small amount of the market output.

B. A company produces a unique product for which there is no easy substitute.

C. A company has no control over price.

D. Buyers have all of the information they need about price, quality, and product availability.

14. Another term for monopoly is

A. competitor

B. marketplace

C. capital

D. trust

Factors of Production   Lesson 5.2

This lesson will help you understand the four factors of production that make all markets work. Use it with core lesson 5.2 Factors of Production to reinforce and apply your knowledge.

Key Concept
The factors of production, which include natural resources, labor, capital, and entrepreneurship, are used to produce goods and services.

Core Skills & Practices
- Analyze Ideas
- Make Inferences

Scarcity and Choice

We all have needs and wants, things we must have to survive and other things that we would enjoy having. However, we have a limited amount of money to spend on both. How do we choose?

Directions: Read the following questions. Then select the correct answer.

1. Scarcity is usually understood as the rarity or short supply of something. In economics, however, scarcity depends on two criteria. What are they?

   A. ease of production and price

   B. natural resources and cost of goods

   C. less supply than demand and the product has value

   D. more supply than demand and the product has value

2. A video game that sold for $49.95 when it came out now sells for $9.95 two years later. What most likely caused this drop in price?

   A. poor marketing of the product

   B. production of the game exceeded the demand

   C. high demand for the product drove prices down

   D. the opportunity cost was too high

Directions: Answer questions 3 and 4 based on the scenario below:

> Your cell phone has stopped working and you need to buy a new one. Two models offer the same benefits, but one costs $50 more than the other. You wanted to use that $50 to take a friend to her favorite restaurant for her birthday. After reading the reviews of both phone models, you choose the more expensive one and decide to make a nice dinner at home for your friend.

3. What is the opportunity cost of this decision?

   A. taking your friend to a restaurant

   B. getting a better phone for more money

   C. making her birthday dinner at home

   D. spending $50 more than you wanted to spend

4. In the scenario above, you based your decision more on _____ than on need.

   A. phone price

   B. phone model

   C. want

   D. opportunity cost

Natural and Human Resources

Two of the four factors of production involve natural resources and human resources.

5. Which of the following is NOT a factor of production?

A. human resources

B. capital resources

C. entrepreneurship

D. stock values

6. Which factor of production is most dependent on human creativity?

A. human resources

B. natural resources

C. capital resources

D. entrepreneurship

Directions: Use the passage below to answer questions 7 through 10.

> In the 1830s, Samuel Colt invented the Colt revolver. This gun could be fired six times without reloading. Many people claim that it helped the United States settle the West. Colt had a plan for manufacturing his guns. He explained his idea in a letter to his father:
>
> "The first workman would receive two or three of the most important parts, and would affix these together and pass them on to the next who would do the same, and so on until the complete [revolver] is put together. It would then be inspected and given the finishing touches by experts and each [gun] would be exactly alike and all of its parts would be the same. The workmen, by constant practice in a single operation, would become highly skilled and at the same time very quick and expert at their particular task. So you have better guns and more of them for less money than if you hire men and have each one make the entire [revolver]."
>
> Quoted in *Yankee Arms Maker: The Incredible Career of Samuel Colt,* by Jack Rohan (Harper & Bros., 1935).

7. Which factor of production was the main focus of Samuel Colt's idea?

A. natural resources

B. human resources

C. relative scarcity

D. supply and demand

8. With Colt's method, more _____ could be made with fewer workers.

9. Why did he think this method would improve productivity?

A. The workers would take more pride in their work.

B. The value of the product would rise in the market.

C. The quality and the speed of production would increase.

D. The cost of production would be less dependent on natural resources.

10. The name for the working method developed by Samuel Colt is _____.

✓ Test-Taking Tip

During a test, as you are reading a question, circle or write key words that help you understand what the question is asking.

11. Complete the chart below by identifying each resource as **renewable** or **nonrenewable**.

Resource	Renewable	Nonrenewable
Grains		
Natural gas		
Cotton		
Paper		
Coal		
Land		

Capital and Entrepreneurship

Combining capital resources with natural resources and labor results in more goods and services produced.

Questions: Read the passage below. Then answer questions 12 and 13.

> In 1902 Hershey began producing its famous "KISSES® candy pieces." Each individual KISS® was wrapped by hand. Then in 1921, an invention called a channel wrapper made this labor-intensive part of the process much faster.

12. The introduction of the channel wrapper by the Hershey company directly affected which of the following?

    A. natural resources

    B. capital resources

    C. aluminum supply

    D. chocolate supply

13. A manufacturer best handles rationing—the regulation of quantities and kinds of goods bought, sold, and traded—by:

    A. reducing the labor force.

    B. stopping production until the rationing is lifted.

    C. increasing his capital costs by adding new machinery.

    D. finding alternative natural resources that work well

Directions: Use the map below to answer questions 14 and 15.

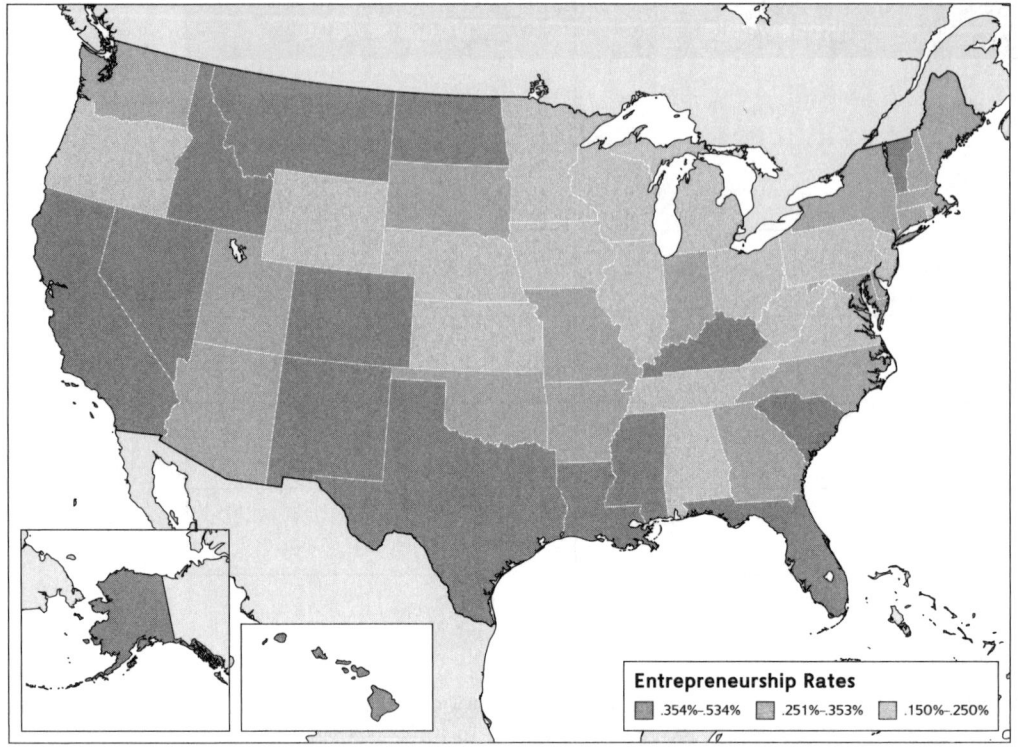

Data shown indicate the number of businesses per 100,000 adults in each state. For example, in 2012 there were 530 businesses per 100,000 people in the state of Montana (rate = 0.53).

14. States in which automobile manufacturing and mining have been a large part of their economies (e.g., Michigan, Ohio, Pennsylvania, Wisconsin, etc.) are shown in the lightest color. Which economic factor probably plays the greatest role in those states having less entrepreneurship than other states?

    A. lack of natural resources

    B. lack of appropriately trained labor for new ventures

    C. fewer wealthy leaders to provide capital

    D. lack of transportation resources

15. Which region of the United States has the lowest rates of entrepreneurship?

    A. the west coast and south

    B. the south and east coast

    C. the mid-west and northeast

    D. the north east and west coast

Profits and Productivity Lesson 5.3

This lesson will help you understand how businesses can increase profits and productivity. Use it with core lesson 5.3 Profits and Productivity to reinforce and apply your knowledge.

Key Concept

The possibility of increased profits is an incentive for business owners to take risks, to expand, and to try various strategies that will increase productivity.

Core Skills & Practices

- Interpret Graphics
- Use Context Clues to Understand Meaning

Risks and Profits

Businesses are willing to take risks to make a profit. A profit is money earned after all expenses are paid. A profit is also how much better off someone is after they buy or sell a good or service.

Directions: Read the following questions. Then select the correct answer.

1. Profit is the difference between

   A. income from sales and expenses.
   B. income and investments.
   C. cash on hand and savings.
   D. wages and sales.

2. Which of the following would boost a company's current level of productivity?

   A. labor shortage
   B. research and development
   C. increasing capital and human and natural resources
   D. decreasing capital and human and natural resources

3. Wages, interest payments, tools, office supplies, packaging, electricity, telephone service, postage, and transportation costs are business

   A. profits.
   B. losses.
   C. expenses.
   D. wages.

4. Steve Jobs, co-founder and former CEO of Apple, developed and produced new computer technology. What is he considered to be?

   A. a broker
   B. a capitalist
   C. an economist
   D. an entrepreneur

Directions: Study the chart below, and answer questions 5 through 7.

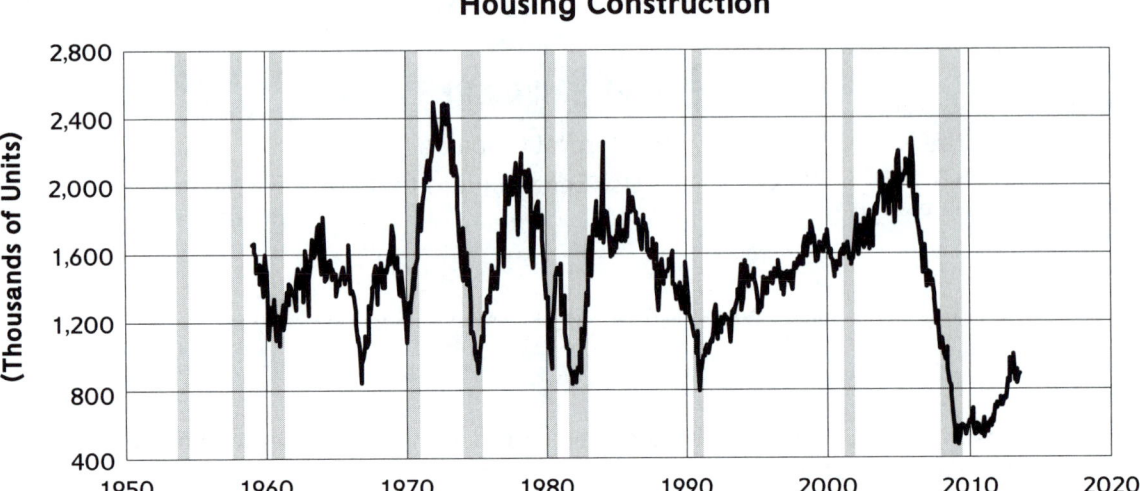

5. According to the chart, the worst year for new housing units started was in _____.

6. Historically, the chart shows that the greatest risk for a home builder is the

   A. threat of a recession.

   B. declining number of houses on the market.

   C. rising cost of materials.

   D. period of time that it takes to construct a house.

7. If you were a new home builder, why would 1995 have been a good year to have gone into business?

   A. The recession of 2002 was over.

   B. The number of purchased homes was decreasing.

   C. The recession of 1990 was smaller than the previous recession.

   D. People were purchasing new houses at an ever-increasing rate.

Test-Taking Tip

To answer questions related to a chart or graph, first carefully read the title. Then identify the units that are used in plotting the chart or graph. Finally, determine the trend, conditions, or measurements that the chart or graph is attempting to show.

Productivity and Profits

One way that businesses increase profits is through productivity. Developing better ways to produce goods and services costs some time and resources, but it usually pays off in the long term.

Directions: Read the following questions. Then select the correct answer.

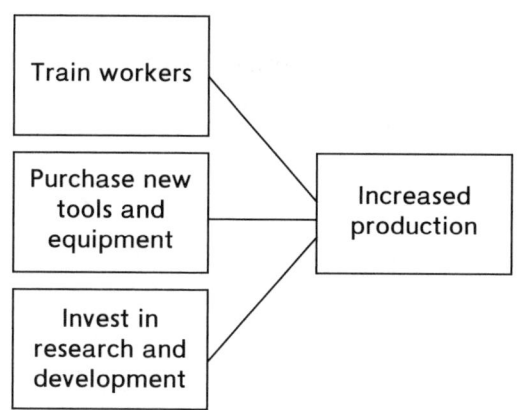

8. What is the opportunity cost associated with the graphic shown here?

    A. an increase in available capital

    B. a decrease in goods and an increase in services produced

    C. a temporary increase in output

    D. a temporary drop in current production

9. Which of the following does not impact productivity?

    A. research and development

    B. employee training programs

    C. decreasing capital investments

    D. upgrading technology

Directions: Use the following table to answer questions 10 and 11.

Global Top Ten Firms Spending on Research and Development in 2010

1. Roche Holding global health care $9.1 billion
2. Microsoft software, electronics $9 billion
3. Nokia telecommunications $8.2 billion
4. Toyota automobiles $7.8 billion
5. Pfizer pharmaceuticals $7.7 billion
6. Novartis pharmaceuticals $7.5 billion
7. Johnson & Johnson pharmaceutical $7 billion
8. Sanofi Aventis pharmaceuticals $6.3 billion
9. Glaxo Smith Kline pharmaceuticals $6.2 billion
10. Samsung electronics $6 billion

Source: *The Christian Science Monitor* http://www.csmonitor.com/Business/2010/1115/R-D-spending-Here-are-the-Top-10-firms/Samsung

2014 GED® Test Exercise Book

10. Which group of companies spends the most on research and development?

   A. electronics

   B. automobiles

   C. pharmaceuticals

   D. global health care

11. What justifies such large expenses for research and development in the pharmaceutical companies?

   A. potential earnings from patented new medicines

   B. the rising cost of health care

   C. the number of people in the electronics market

   D. the lack of serious competition

Incentives and Risk Taking

Individuals and businesses are more willing to take risks and invest in their new products if they are encouraged to do so with incentives.

Directions: Read the following questions. Then select the correct answers.

12. In a free market economy, the encouragement to try new ideas or invent new products is called

   A. incentive.

   B. profit.

   C. monopoly.

   D. opportunity cost.

13. Today no modern country has which of the following kinds of economic system?

   A. command

   B. traditional

   C. free market

   D. mixed

14. In the United States, the government has the right to take away a person's property if the government does what?

   A. The government owns the property, so it doesn't have to do anything.

   B. The government can just take the property by force.

   C. The government must arrest the owner.

   D. The government must pay the owner.

Directions: Read the following paragraph, and use the word bank to fill in the missing words.

goods and services   **incentives**   **economic growth**   **command**

15. By the end of the twentieth century, several countries that had _____ economies began to offer more free market incentives. Russia, China, and India opened opportunities for individuals to own businesses. Only a few primarily command economies remained, including North Korea, Cuba, and Iran. Increased economic freedom and opportunity gave people _____ to produce more _____. Workers contributed more because they were rewarded for it. As a result, these countries experienced _____.

Specialization and Comparative Advantage Lesson 5.4

This lesson will help you understand how and why businesses decide what they are going to produce by looking at what other companies produce. Use it with core lesson 5.4 Specialization and Comparative Advantage to reinforce and apply your knowledge.

Key Concept
Specialization increases productivity and provides businesses with a comparative advantage but also leads to interdependence.

Core Skills & Practices
- Gather Information
- Identify Facts and Details

Specialization

Specialization is when a company decides to focus on making only a few goods or providing a limited number of services, helping the company become more profitable because it finds ways to be very efficient.

Directions: Read the following question. Then select the correct answer.

1. An absolute advantage is the ability to produce a product or service using _____ resources than other producers require.

   A. fever

   B. higher

   C. human

   D. specialization

Directions: Use the graphic organizer below to answer question 2.

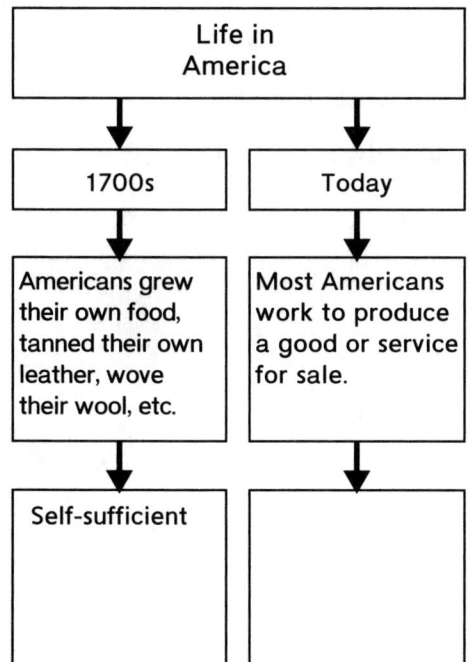

2. Which word best fills in the empty box?

   A. specialize

   B. opportunity cost

   C. absolute advantage

   D. comparative advantage

Directions: Read the passage below. Then answer the questions that follow.

> With more than a century of growing potatoes, Idaho has produced more than any other state every year since 1957, producing around 30 percent of the US fall production per year. Bingham County produces almost more potatoes than the entire state of Maine! Potatoes contribute more than $2 billion, or approximately 15%, of Idaho's gross state product.
>
> —Idaho State Department of Education

3. Which of the following statements best describes Idaho's market position in potatoes?

   A. Idaho has a higher comparative advantage in growing potatoes.

   B. Idaho enjoys an absolute advantage in growing potatoes.

   C. Idaho is the only state that grows potatoes.

   D. Idaho potatoes taste better than other varieties.

4. In order to produce so many potatoes, farmers in Idaho must be very

   A. thrifty.

   B. efficient.

   C. resourceful.

   D. opportunistic.

Comparative Advantage

Individuals and businesses with a comparative advantage specialize in goods or services that are produced at a relatively low opportunity cost, that is, more easily than other companies could do so.

Directions: Read the questions below. Then select the correct answers.

5. Company A and Company B both make mops and brooms. If Company A can make more mops and brooms than Company B, it has a higher [1 Select...▼] than Company B. Because Company A makes more mops than brooms, it wants to [2 Select...▼] in mops.

   [1 Select...▼]

   A. monopoly

   B. specialization

   C. absolute advantage

   D. comparative advantage

   [2 Select...▼]

   A. monopoly

   B. specialize

   C. absolute advantage

   D. comparative advantage

6. The law of comparative advantage says that those with the lower opportunity cost should

   A. produce both goods.

   B. produce fewer goods or services.

   C. specialize in a product or service.

   D. seek an absolute advantage.

Directions: Use the chart below to answer questions 7–10.

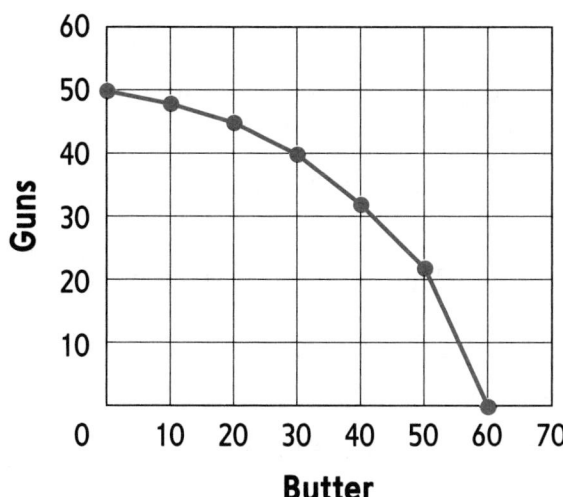

Production of Guns and Butter

7. How many guns could be produced if no butter is produced?

   A. 50

   B. 60

   C. 70

   D. 80

8. If the same producer made both guns and butter, what is the maximum number of these items that could be produced?

   A. 60

   B. 110

   C. more than 50

   D. fewer than 70

9. By specializing and producing those items for which they had a comparative advantage, separate gun producers and butter producers could together produce _____ total butter and guns.

   A. 100

   B. 105

   C. 110

   D. 120

10. When 40 guns are produced then _____ butter are produced.

✓ Test-Taking Tip

When using a graph to answer a question, make sure you understand what information is being presented. Try writing down the information listed on the x and y-axes on a sheet of scrap paper. It may also help to use a straight edge, like the side of a pencil, to read information on the graph.

Interdependence

When businesses are linked to other businesses to operate, they are said to be interdependent.

Directions: Read the following questions. Then select the correct answers.

11. Interdependence occurs when producers rely on one another for information, _____, goods, and resources.

    A. services

    B. productivity

    C. specialization

    D. opportunity costs

12. Which of the following is not true about interdependence?

    A. Companies can share resources through specialization.

    B. Interdependence goes hand in hand with specialization.

    C. Companies can share resources through interdependence.

    D. Negative events in one country have little to no effect on other countries.

13. What benefits would help a producer minimize the risk that interdependence poses?

    A. Increased profitability results from increased trade.

    B. Decreased profitability results in decreased competition.

    C. Increased specialization results in increased productivity.

    D. Decreased specialization results in increased trade.

Microeconomics Lesson 6.1

This lesson will help you understand how the economic behavior of individuals and companies can be analyzed. Use it with core lesson 6.1 Microeconomics to reinforce and apply your knowledge.

Key Concept
The forces of supply and demand determine the market prices of most products and resources in the US and global economies.

Core Skills & Practices
- Analyze Information
- Use Maps, Charts, and Graphs

Market Influences

Directions: Read the following questions. Then select the correct answer.

1. The study of market exchanges between buyers and sellers is called _____.

   A. economy
   B. mixed economy
   C. microeconomics
   D. macroeconomics

2. Which of the following statements best describes how prices are set?

   A. Sellers set prices for goods and services.
   B. Buyers set prices for goods and services.
   C. Manufacturers set prices for goods; workers set prices for services.
   D. Sellers set prices, but buyers influence price changes.

3. Complete the table below, using the following terms.

   | prices | demand | supply |

   | command economy | mixed economy |

	The amount of goods and services buyers are willing and able to buy
	Government regulation of parts of the market
	A signal to buyers and sellers
	The amount of goods and services a producer is willing and able to produce
	Government control of the market

2014 GED® Test Exercise Book

Directions: Read the following questions. Then select the correct answer.

4. Which of the following occurs when prices rise?

   A. signals buyers to stock up on an item

   B. signals producers to slow production

   C. signals producers to increase production

   D. signals producers to specialize in one product

5. Which of the following occurs when prices fall?

   A. signals buyers to delay a purchase

   B. signals producers to slow production

   C. signals producers to increase production

   D. signals producers to specialize in one product

Laws of Supply and Demand

Supply is the amount of goods and services available. Demand describes how much consumers desire a product. The two concepts are related in a free market economy.

Directions: Use the chart below to answer questions 6–9.

The Demand for CDs

6. How many CDs would be demanded at a price of $9?

   A. 3

   B. 5

   C. 8

   D. 10

7. When the price for CDs is 3, the quantity demanded is _____.

8. Between which two prices did market demand increase the most?

   A. $18–$15

   B. $12–$9

   C. $9–$6

   D. $6–$3

9. When 5 CDs are demanded the price is _____.

Directions: Use the chart below to answer question 10.

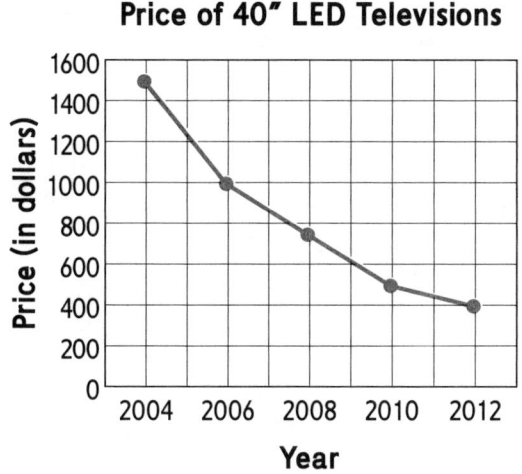

10. If the price rises, the quantity supplied also rises. If the price drops, the quantity supplied goes down as well. What explains this?

   A. People do not usually buy in bulk.

   B. Prices are not always a good signal.

   C. The profit motive drives suppliers.

   D. Sales generate more business.

Directions: Use the graph below to answer question 11.

11. Look at the graphs. Circle the graph that demonstrates a supply curve.

12. Identify each statement as either *buyer* or *seller*.

buyer	seller

The demand curve relates to the _____.

The supply curve relates to the _____.

A consumer is also known as the _____.

A producer is also known as the _____.

2014 GED® Test Exercise Book

Market Equilibrium

The aim of the market is to compromise between the interests of the buyers and the interests of the sellers. Market equilibrium is reached when demand is equal to the supply.

Directions: Use the chart below to answer questions 13 and 14.

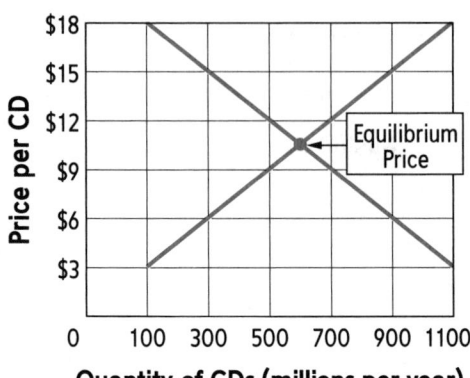

13. The equilibrium price is where the quantity demanded meets the

    A. price demanded.

    B. price supplied.

    C. supply demanded.

    D. quantity supplied.

14. How many CDs will be sold at the equilibrium price?

    A. 500 million

    B. 600 million

    C. 700 million

    D. 800 million

 Test-Taking Tip

When trying to determine the correct answer to a multiple-choice question, begin by deciding the correct answer before looking at the answer choices. Then, match the answer you believe to be correct with one of the possible choices.

Macroeconomics and Government Policy   Lesson 6.2

This lesson will help you understand how our government forms and carries out policies that affect the nation's economy. Use it with core lesson 6.2 Macroeconomics and Government Policy to reinforce and apply your knowledge.

Key Concept
The federal government uses fiscal policies and monetary policies to manage the economy.

Core Skills & Practices
- Identify Comparisons and Contrasts
- Interpret Meaning

Federal Revenue and Expenditures

The federal government collects income, mostly from taxes, so it is able to perform its business and pay for its expenses.

Directions: Read the following questions. Then select the correct answers.

1. Approximately half of the government's income, or revenue, comes from

   A. tariffs.

   B. user fees.

   C. income taxes.

   D. property taxes.

2. How does the government borrow money from American citizens?

   A. placing tariffs on imports

   B. selling bonds to individuals

   C. collecting personal income taxes

   D. collecting Medicare payroll deductions

3. The government borrows money by selling bonds and other securities to individuals and businesses. When you buy a savings bond, you are _____ the government money.

   A. rewarding

   B. stealing

   C. loaning

   D. saving

4. How might a subsidy on corn affect consumers?

   A. It would decrease the supply of corn.

   B. It would change the quality of the corn.

   C. It would reduce the cost of corn to consumers.

   D. It would increase the cost of corn to consumers.

Directions: Use the chart below to answer questions 5 and 6.

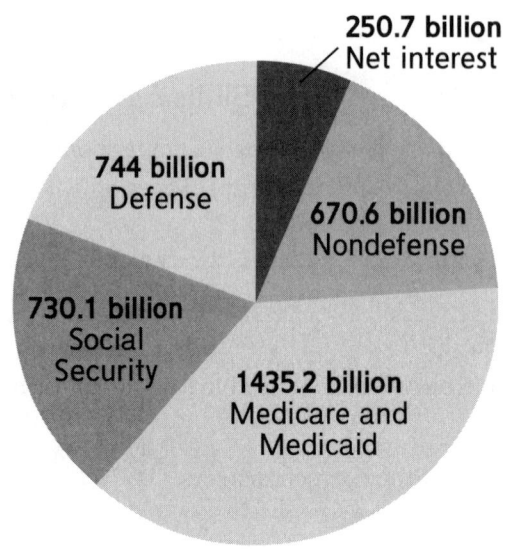

Fiscal Year 2011 Budget Request

- 250.7 billion Net interest
- 744 billion Defense
- 670.6 billion Nondefense
- 730.1 billion Social Security
- 1435.2 billion Medicare and Medicaid

5. Rank the 2011 proposed budget expenditures by category from highest spending to lowest spending. Write the expenditure in the correct box.

1.	Nondefense
2.	Social Security
3.	Interest
4.	Medicare/Medicaid
5.	Defense

6. One effect of the 2011 stimulus spending was that the national deficit increased to

   A. $5.8 trillion.

   B. $1.5 trillion.

   C. $834 billion.

   D. $300 billion.

Federal Fiscal and Monetary Policies

To manage its economy effectively, the federal government must have specific plans related to revenue, money supply, credit, and interest rates.

Directions: Read the following questions. Then select the correct answer.

7. Tariffs are taxes on _____.

   A. quotas

   B. exports

   C. imports

   D. goods and services

8. Governments use _____ to limit the amount of goods that can be brought into a country during a specific period.

   A. quotas

   B. exports

   C. imports

   D. goods and services

10. What was the intent behind the Federal Reserve Act of 1913?

    A. to protect consumers

    B. to enhance economic competition

    C. to subsidize farms

    D. to stabilize the economy

11. Which of the following can cause market failures?

    A. bank closings because of panics

    B. imperfect competition

    C. gaps between private costs and social costs of behaviors

    D. wrong Fed decisions

Directions: Use the chart below to answer question 9.

9. Complete the chart below by writing the correct purpose in the column next to each policy.

   - to promote a particular business
   - to promote economic growth
   - to slow economic activity or reduce inflation
   - to protect American businesses from foreign competition

Policy	Purpose
provide a subsidy	
increase interest rates	
enact a tariff	
put money into circulation	

✓ Test-Taking Tip

If you can't identify all the correct answers in a drag-and-drop activity, begin with the one or two that you know. Eliminate the choices that you know are incorrect, and then select the best option from the remaining choices. Blank answer spaces will count against your overall score.

2014 GED® Test Exercise Book

Directions: Read the excerpt below. Then answer the questions that follow.

> "In short, the original goal of the Great Experiment that was the founding of the Fed was the preservation of financial stability...How should a central bank enhance financial stability? One means is by assuming the lender-of-last-resort function...under which the central bank uses its power to provide liquidity to ease market conditions during periods of panic or incipient panic...However, putting out the fire is not enough; it is also important to foster a financial system that is sufficiently resilient to withstand large financial shocks. Toward that end, the Federal Reserve, together with other regulatory agencies...is actively engaged in monitoring financial developments and working to strengthen financial institutions and markets...What about the monetary policy framework? In general, the Federal Reserve's policy framework...include[s an] emphasis on preserving the Fed's inflation credibility, which is critical for anchoring inflation expectation."
>
> —Chairman Ben S. Bernanke at "The First 100 Years of the Federal Reserve: The Policy Record, Lessons Learned, and Prospects for the Future," a conference sponsored by the National Bureau of Economic Research, Cambridge, Massachusetts, July 10, 2013

12. The primary goal of the Federal Reserve is to

    A. control the nations' banks.

    B. monitor financial developments.

    C. prevent inflation.

    D. preserve financial stability.

13. The Federal Reserve's "power of liquidity" is its

    A. control over the money supply.

    B. ability to flow in any direction.

    C. number of reserve banks.

    D. independence from the executive and legislative branches.

14. During good economic times, the Fed will pursue policies designed to

    A. reduce interest rates as low as possible.

    B. control inflation as much as possible.

    C. regulate financial institutions as little as possible.

    D. increase liquidity when available.

Directions: Read the writing prompt below. Then write your answer on a separate sheet of paper.

15. On a separate sheet of paper, explain the four functions of the Federal Reserve System and its role in the nation's economy.

Macroeconomics, the GDP, and Price Fluctuation Lesson 6.3

This lesson will help you understand how a variety of measures help measure the health of an economy. Use it with core lesson 6.3 Macroeconomics, the GDP, and Price Fluctuation to reinforce and apply your knowledge.

Key Concept

Measures such as an economy's GDP, inflation or deflation rate, and unemployment rate provide economists with ways to measure an economy's health.

Core Skills & Practices

- Read Charts
- Integrate Visual Information

GDP

Gross domestic product, the value of all goods and services produced in the nation in a year, is one of the most vital measurements of a nation's economy.

Directions: Read the following questions. Then select the correct answers.

1. GDP stands for _____ and is a measure of the dollar value of all final goods and services produced in the United States during the year.

   A. general domestic production

   B. gross economic product

   C. good domestic production

   D. gross domestic product

2. In which of these countries would GDP be the least useful measure of the strength of the economy?

   A. an island nation, where bartering is common

   B. a tiny nation that is part of the European Union

   C. a large Asian nation with a strong government

   D. a nation that participates in United States trade agreements

Directions: Use the chart below to answer question 3.

Country	GDP in 2012 (in trillion $)
Canada	1.8
China	8.4
Mexico	1.2
United Kingdom	2.4
United States	15.7

3. Which country has a GDP that is approximately twice the GDP of Mexico?

   A. Canada

   B. China

   C. United Kingdom

   D. United States

2014 GED® Test Exercise Book

Directions: Use the chart below to answer question 4.

4. Write the name of each product in the correct category to show whether or not it would count toward US GDP.

| Automobiles designed in Japan but produced in South Carolina | California surfboards sold in Mexico | Corn from Iowa sold at the Iowa State Fair |

| Housekeeping performed by a United States homeowner | Natural gas from Canada used in Illinois | Oil from Alaska used in Texas |

| Seats made in the United States, to be installed in a new Buick in Detroit | United States-made snow tires sold separately from a vehicle in San Diego |

Part of US GDP	NOT Part of US GDP

Inflation and Deflation

Inflation and deflation, the rise and fall of prices, affect the GDP in different ways.

Directions: Read the following question. Then select the correct answer.

5. A rise in the general level of prices over time is called _____.

   A. GDP

   B. inflation

   C. deflation

   D. opportunity cost

Test-Taking Tip

When answering fill-in-the-blank questions, consider the part of speech that is missing from the sentence. If a verb is missing, then consider only verbs for the correct response. If a noun is missing, then consider only nouns.

Directions: Use the graph below to answer questions 6–8.

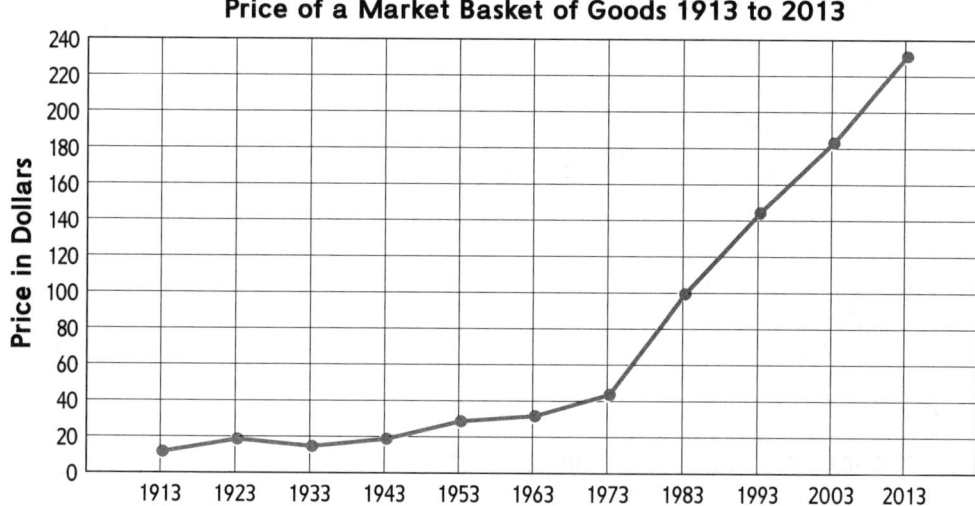

6. In 1973, the price of a market basket of goods was _____.

7. The graph is a visual representation of inflation and deflation in the American economy. During which of these years was there a period of deflation in the United States?

A. 1923

B. 1933

C. 1943

D. 1953

8. The Federal Reserve believes that 2 percent inflation is desirable. At that rate, approximately how much would this market basket of goods most likely cost in 2023?

A. $234.00

B. $245.00

C. $268.00

D. $280.00

Unemployment

Unemployment happens when people leave their former jobs for any number of reasons and have not yet found new jobs.

Directions: Read the following questions. Then select the correct answers.

9. The _____ rate is the percentage of individuals in the civilian labor force who are actively looking for a job but cannot find one.

A. cyclical

B. inflation

C. deflation

D. unemployment

10. Businesses lay off workers during recession and hire them back in good times, causing _____ unemployment.

A. cyclical

B. seasonal

C. structural

D. technological

2014 GED® Test Exercise Book

Directions: Use the graph to answer questions 11–14.

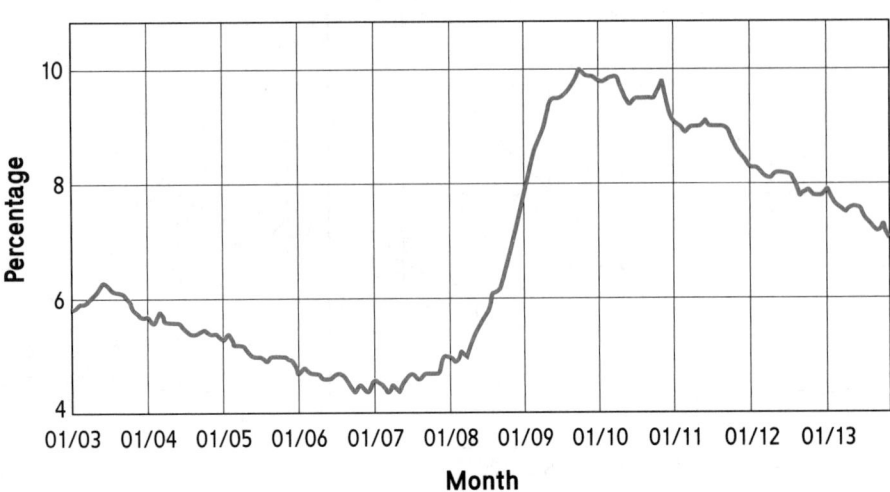

Source: http://data.bls.gov/timeseries/LNS14000000

11. During which year represented in the graph was the American unemployment rate highest?

   A. 2008
   B. 2009
   C. 2010
   D. 2012

12. Toward the end of 2009, the unemployment rate peaked at _____ percent.

13. What was the approximate difference in unemployment rate between the beginning of 2003 and the beginning of 2013?

   A. + 2 percent
   B. + 4 percent
   C. – 1 percent
   D. – 2 percent

14. The unemployment rate in January 2009 was _____ percent.

Major Economic Events Lesson 7.1

This lesson will help you understand major economic events in American history. Use it with core lesson 7.1 Major Economic Events to reinforce and apply your knowledge.

Key Concept
The federal government has responded to economic events in a variety of ways; for example, by developing stimulus programs and regulating businesses.

Core Skills & Practices
- Analyze Information
- Identify Point of View

Booms and Busts

Throughout its history, the United States has experienced economic booms and busts.

Directions: Complete the following paragraph with the correct terms.

1. Businesses hire workers during an economic _____, and the economy can experience _____. Businesses lose money and lay off workers during an economic _____. During a low point in the business cycle, the economy can experience _____.

Directions: Read the following questions. Then select the correct answers.

2. Mass production had what effect on the economy in the 1920s?

   A. It caused the unemployment rate to increase.

   B. It lowered the prices of goods significantly.

   C. It allowed an increase in middle-class families.

   D. It caused a trough to develop in the economy.

3. At a certain point, an increased demand for Model Ts would lead to a drop in supply. At that point, which of these is likely to have happened?

   A. an increase in price

   B. a decrease in inflation

   C. a decline in GDP

   D. an economic trough

4. The years 1920 to 1929 would be considered a time of economic _____ in the United States.

   A. bust

   B. boom

   C. recession

   D. depression

The Great Depression

The Great Depression was a period of severe decline in the US economy during the 1930s.

Directions: Complete the following paragraph with the correct terms.

5. Wealth in the 1920s was mainly based on the value of _____. When people bought stock, they bought it on _____, paying only about 10% and borrowing the rest. When the stock market plummeted on _____, many investors lost all their savings. Other citizens lost savings when _____ failed.

Directions: Use the passage to answer questions 5–8.

> During the period between 1929 and 1933, more than 100,000 businesses failed, causing massive job losses. Without employment, many families lost their homes. With almost 25% of American workers out of work and homeless, shantytowns began to appear in parks and at the edges of cities. These collections of shacks were called "Hoovervilles." Although Hoovervilles were made of temporary and makeshift structures, some were organized, with a mayor and governing committees. Even after the Great Depression, Hoovervilles persisted in some areas.

6. Large shantytowns populated by the unemployed and homeless appeared as a result of

   A. Black Tuesday.

   B. the Great Depression.

   C. the Roaring Twenties.

   D. the Hooverville boom.

7. Why were the shantytowns named Hoovervilles?

   A. President Hoover had enacted many government programs that provided economic relief to individuals.

   B. President Hoover had been involved in the stock market crash, which had damaged the economy.

   C. Many companies owned by Herbert Hoover had failed, increasing unemployment during the Great Depression.

   D. Massive unemployment and foreclosures occurred during Herbert Hoover's tenure as president.

8. What is the most likely reason Hoovervilles would have persisted beyond the Great Depression?

   A. Strong communities were formed in these shantytowns.

   B. Some Hooverville governments were highly effective.

   C. Some people preferred living outside to living inside.

   D. Relief programs took time to help all those who were in need.

The Government Responds

The federal government implemented laws and set up agencies to combat economic hardship and pull the United States out of the Great Depression.

Directions: Answer the following question.

9. Complete the table on the right by writing the purpose of each New Deal program next to its name and acronym.

Description
Built dams and power plants in the South
Hired people to complete construction projects
Hired people to plant forests
Insured money people deposited in banks
Paid farmers to produce fewer crops
Regulated how much businesses could produce

Program	Description
Agricultural Adjustment Administration (AAA)	
Civilian Conservation Corps (CCC)	
Fair Labor Standards Act (FLSA)	
National Recovery Administration (NRA)	
Tennessee Valley Authority (TVA)	
Works Progress Administration (WPA)	

Directions: Use the passage below to answer questions 10–12.

(1) Our greatest primary task is to put people to work. (2) This is no unsolvable problem if we face it wisely and courageously. (3) It can be accomplished in part by direct recruiting by the Government itself, treating the task as we would treat the emergency of a war, but at the same time, through this employment, accomplishing greatly needed projects to stimulate and reorganize the use of our natural resources…(4) The task can be helped by definite efforts to raise the values of agricultural products and with this the power to purchase the output of our cities. (5) It can be helped by preventing realistically the tragedy of the growing loss through foreclosure of our small homes and our farms. (6) It can be helped by insistence that the Federal, State, and local governments act forthwith on the demand that their cost be drastically reduced. (7) It can be helped by the unifying of relief activities which today are often scattered, uneconomical, and unequal. (8) It can be helped by national planning for and supervision of all forms of transportation and of communications and other utilities which have a definitely public character. (9) There are many ways in which it can be helped, but it can never be helped merely by talking about it. (10) We must act and act quickly.

—President Franklin D. Roosevelt, First Inaugural Address, 1933

10. In which sentence does Roosevelt speak of an issue that would be partially addressed by the creation of Social Security?

    A. sentence 4

    B. sentence 5

    C. sentence 7

    D. sentence 8

11. New Deal programs outlined in Roosevelt's speech provided _____ to the economy by providing relief to workers and reforms for businesses.

12. Which of these statements summarizes Roosevelt's point of view, as outlined in his speech?

    A. The government must control all aspects of the American economy.

    B. The economy can be improved through government intervention.

    C. Direct monetary relief is the only way to help the poorest Americans.

    D. Local and state governments are corrupt and must be reined in.

 Test-Taking Tip

Fill-in-the-blank questions are often used to test your knowledge of vocabulary words. Answering these questions will be easier if you study the accepted definition for each vocabulary word in a lesson or chapter.

The Relationship Between Politics and Economics Lesson 7.2

This lesson will help you explain the relationship between political and economic freedoms, identify the economic causes and impacts of wars, and discuss how exploration and colonization were driven by economic factors. Use it with core lesson 7.2 The Relationship Between Politics and Economics to reinforce and apply your knowledge.

Key Concept
Politics and economics interact with each other in complex ways that affect the entire society.

Core Skills & Practices
- Compare and Contrast
- Make Inferences

Political and Economic Freedom
In the United States, the balance between personal freedom, as outlined in the Constitution, and economic freedom is frequently addressed.

Directions: Use the passage below to answer questions 1 and 2.

> The time is arriving when we can have further tax reduction, when, unless we wish to hamper the people in their right to earn a living, we must have tax reform. The method of raising revenue ought not to impede the transaction of business; it ought to encourage it. I am opposed to extremely high rates, because they produce little or no revenue, because they are bad for the country, and, finally, because they are wrong. We cannot finance the country, we cannot improve social conditions, through any system of injustice, even if we attempt to inflict it upon the rich. Those who suffer the most harm will be the poor. This country believes in prosperity. It is absurd to suppose that it is envious of those who are already prosperous. The wise and correct course to follow in taxation and all other economic legislation is not to destroy those who have already secured success but to create conditions under which everyone will have a better chance to be successful.
>
> —President Calvin Coolidge, Inaugural Address, 1925

1. The speech indicates that President Calvin Coolidge had a _____ approach to government.

   A. laissez-faire

   B. reductionist

   C. totalitarian

   D. socialist

2. Which of these statements does the speech appear to support?

   A. The poor will benefit most from larger taxes on the rich.

   B. Prosperity cannot be attained unless taxation is increased.

   C. Successful people should not be punished through taxation.

   D. The tax system should be completely abolished in the United States.

3. Which of these is an inference about Coolidge's beliefs that can be made from this speech?

    A. Poor people have been treated justly.

    B. Rich people earned their success.

    C. Taxation is completely unnecessary.

    D. Poor people are jealous of rich people.

Directions: Complete the following paragraph with the correct terms.

4. President Franklin D. Roosevelt used the ideas of _____, a noted economist, to create the _____ plan. This plan increased _____ involvement in all aspects of the economy. Programs managed by the government have been used since the Great Depression, during periods of _____.

The Politics of Imperialism

The policy of imperialism—the governing of weaker nations or colonies by more powerful nations—is an example of the influence of politics on the economy.

Directions: Use the chart below to answer question 5.

5. Complete the table by writing each of the four terms below next to the correct description.

| Annexation | Open Door Policy |
| Imperialism | Tariff |

Description	
Hawaii was added to the United States as a territory in 1898.	
Sugar from Brazil is taxed when it enters the United States.	
The United States and Mexico both have the right to trade with China.	
The United States obtains territory to build a canal in Panama.	

Directions: Read the following question. Then select the correct answer.

6. One root of American _____ in the late 1800s was an overabundance of American goods.

   A. socialism

   B. democracy

   C. imperialism

   D. laissez-faire

Directions: Read the passage below. Then answer the questions that follow.

> I, Liliuokalani of Hawaii, by the will of God named heir apparent on the tenth day of April, A.D. 1877, and by the grace of God Queen of the Hawaiian Islands on the seventeenth day of January, A.D. 1893, do hereby protest against the ratification of a certain treaty, which, so I am informed, has been signed at Washington by Messrs. Hatch, Thurston, and Kinney, purporting to cede those Islands to the territory and dominion of the United States. I declare such a treaty to be an act of wrong toward the native and part-native people of Hawaii, an invasion of the rights of the ruling chiefs, in violation of international rights both toward my people and toward friendly nations with whom they have made treaties, the perpetuation of the fraud whereby the constitutional government was overthrown, and, finally, an act of gross injustice to me.
>
> —Queen Liliuokalani of Hawaii, Official Protest to the Treaty of Annexation, 1897

7. What does Queen Liliuokalani imply about her role as ruler of Hawaii?

   A. She was ordained by God to rule.

   B. She was chosen by the people to rule.

   C. She supports American rule of Hawaii.

   D. She needs help from the US government.

8. Why does Queen Liliuokalani protest the treaty referred to in the passage?

   A. It gives native Hawaiians more say in their government.

   B. It ignores the right of Hawaii to rule itself independently.

   C. It spreads imperialism into the South Pacific region.

   D. It overthrows the constitutional government of Hawaii.

✓ Test-Taking Tip

An inference is a conclusion that is reached on the basis of evidence and reasoning. When you are asked to identify an inference based on evidence from a reading passage, first read the inferences that are provided. Then read the passage to see which inference could be made based on information in the passage.

The Economics of War

War and conflict are sometimes the result of countries attempting to gain or control natural resources.

Directions: Read the following question. Then select the correct answer.

9. Which of these impacts of war could indirectly cause homelessness?

    A. War disrupts businesses.

    B. Bombing destroys houses.

    C. Fighting destroys farm fields.

    D. Conflict shuts down power grids.

Directions: Read the passage below. Then answer the questions that follow.

> The United States has a long history of extending a helping hand to people overseas struggling to make a better life. It is a history that both reflects the American people's compassion and support of human dignity as well as advances US foreign policy interests.
>
> —US Agency for International Development, Statement of "Who We Are"

10. US Agency for International Development provides _____ aid to improve the lives of people in foreign countries that may have been affected by war or famine.

11. How would US aid advance US foreign policy interests?

    A. by stabilizing economies of foreign countries

    B. by providing military support to foreign countries

    C. by showing that US citizens can be compassionate

    D. by supporting those who want to overthrow dictators

Directions: Complete the following paragraph with the correct terms..

12. War creates unstable _____, which scare away _____. However, money is needed after a war to rebuild _____, to provide food and services to people who have been affected by war, and to support _____ that are trying to reopen.

The Scientific and Industrial Revolutions Lesson 7.3

This lesson will help you understand how the Scientific and Industrial Revolutions have shaped modern life. Use it with core lesson 7.3 The Scientific and Industrial Revolutions to reinforce and apply your knowledge.

Key Concept
Today's world has been shaped by the technological advances that came about as a result of the Scientific and Industrial Revolutions.

Core Skills & Practices
- Interpret Meaning
- Identify Cause and Effect

The Scientific Revolution

During the Scientific Revolution, which lasted from the late 1500s to the early 1600s, people began to use rational thinking to question old ideas about the world around them and to search for new answers.

Directions: Read the following questions. Then select the correct answers.

1. The _____ is the process used by scientists for testing ideas through experimentation and careful observation.

   A. scientific method
   B. industrial method
   C. Scientific Revolution
   D. urbanization

2. Which of these statements best describes the period of the Scientific Revolution?

   A. Political revolution drove scientific discoveries in many nations.
   B. A mass movement of people occurred from the country to cities.
   C. The use of rational thinking caused many former ideas to be discarded.
   D. Scientists began to accept discoveries that were made in the past.

3. Place each scientist in the correct spot in the left table, to show whether his discoveries related to the solar system or the human body.

Solar System	Human Body

Scientists
Andreas Vesalius
Antonie van Leeuwenhoek
Galileo Galilei
Isaac Newton
Nicholas Copernicus

2014 GED® Test Exercise Book

Directions: Use the passage below to answer questions 4 and 5.

> The astrolabe is an instrument that allows the user to study the position of the Sun and stars to determine time during the day or night and the time of a celestial event. During the 15th and 16th centuries, the Mariner's Astrolabe was developed to measure the height of a celestial body above the horizon.

4. An astrolabe would allow a navigator to determine which of these while sailing in the middle of an ocean?

   A. distance to land

   B. time until sunrise

   C. latitude position

   D. distance between stars

5. The invention of the astrolabe had the greatest effect on which of the following?

   A. the Scientific Revolution

   B. industrialization

   C. European exploration

   D. the work of Copernicus and Galileo

The Industrial Revolution

During the time period known as the Industrial Revolution, machines replaced hand tools in the manufacturing of goods, and many people left their farms to work in factories.

Directions: Read the following questions. Then select the correct answers.

6. People who make candles in their homes to sell to local gift shops are operating a(n)

   A. factory.

   B. illegal business.

   C. cottage industry.

   D. stay-at-home industry.

7. What is the most likely effect of an industrial revolution in a country?

   A. More people are able to work at home.

   B. People move from the cities to rural areas.

   C. The economy shifts from agriculture to manufacturing.

   D. New machines make more expensive goods that are difficult to obtain.

Directions: Use the table below to answer questions 8–10.

Cotton Mills in England, 1838

Location in England	Number of Cotton Mills	Number of Employees
Northwest	1,562	215,556
Northeast	16	1,704
Southwest	1	29
Southeast	19	942

8. Based on the information in this chart, you can conclude that in the first half of the 19th century, northwest England most likely developed a higher concentration of

   A. universities.

   B. middle-class families.

   C. labor unions in the southwest.

   D. railroads.

9. The chart suggests that which area of England may have been least affected by the Industrial Revolution?

   A. the northwest

   B. the northeast

   C. the southwest

   D. the southeast

Directions: Complete the following sentences with the correct terms.

10. According to the table, the cotton industry was _____ in one area of England, with _____ other area(s) as (a) smaller textile center(s).

11. The movement of people from farms to industrial cities appears to have been greatest in _____ England.

Test-taking Tip

When answering questions based on a data table, study the table to determine any trends in the data.

The Rise of Cities

Between 1800 and 1850 there was a significant increase in the number and size of cities in Europe and the United States.

Directions: Read the following questions. Then select the correct answers.

12. Before labor unions formed during the Industrial Revolution, which of these statements was true?

    A. Employers were held responsible for workplace accidents.

    B. Employee wages were based on experience and gender.

    C. Employers operated according to their own set of rules.

    D. Employees working long hours received overtime pay.

13. What led to urbanization during the Industrial Revolution?

    A. the need for factory workers

    B. the abundance of city services

    C. healthy living conditions in the cities

    D. high pay and safe working conditions in city jobs

Directions: Use the passage below to answer questions 14 and 15.

> Textile factories in England used child labor to perform many tasks, such as picking up loose cotton or crawling under machines while they were in motion. Interviews with people who worked in cotton mills as children reveal that they were sometimes forced to work from 12–17 hours at the mill, and were punished if they tried to sit down or rest in any way. Very small children were sought for mill work, because they were cheaper to hire as well as being small and agile.

14. Which of these jobs in a cotton mill would most likely be done by the youngest children?

    A. picking up cotton bales from the floor

    B. running cloth-making machinery

    C. running errands for managers outside the factory

    D. crawling under running machines

15. What does this passage indicate about conditions during the Industrial Revolution?

    A. Poverty was common.

    B. Education was valued.

    C. Children worked short days.

    D. Children were protected.

Savings and Banking Lesson 8.1

This lesson will help you learn what banks do and how you can use them. Use it with core lesson 8.1 Savings and Banking to reinforce and apply your knowledge.

Key Concept
Financial institutions provide consumers with services such as checking and savings accounts to help them manage their money.

Core Skills & Practices
- Analyze Events and Details
- Get Meaning from Context

Banks

Banks provide three basic services: keeping money safe, transferring funds, and loaning money.

Directions: Read the following questions. Then select the correct answers.

1. What three basic services do banks provide?

   A. keeping money safe, charging fees for services, and loaning money

   B. keeping money safe, transferring funds, and charging fees for services

   C. charging fees for services, transferring funds, and loaning money

   D. keeping money safe, transferring funds, and loaning money

2. Banks lend out most of their depositors' money; the rest of the deposits are called

   A. reserves

   B. loans

   C. accounts

   D. cash

Directions: Use the chart below to complete question 3.

3. Complete the chart below by writing the name of the financial institution in the chart next to the reason it was originally created.

	Provide emergency loans for its members
	Help individuals buy homes
	Serve the needs of business

commercial banks   credit unions

savings and loan associations

2014 GED® Test Exercise Book

Types of Banks

Over time, several types of banking institutions arose to serve specific needs. Today most financial institutions serve all those needs.

Directions: Read the questions below. Then select the correct answers.

4. What trend has affected the initial purpose of different financial institutions?

   A. Most financial institutions today offer the same services.

   B. Commercial banks outnumber all other financial institutions combined.

   C. Credit unions require members to live in the same community.

   D. Savings and loans provide most of the money for new home buyers.

5. Consumers generally trust that their banks will not lose their money because

   A. consumers know their local bankers.

   B. banks have unlimited resources.

   C. banks buy insurance to cover losses.

   D. consumers are uninformed about their deposits.

6. How do banks earn a profit?

   A. They charge customers more to borrow money than they pay to customers who save.

   B. They only loan money to individuals and businesses with excellent credit ratings.

   C. They transfer funds to overseas banks who pay greater interest.

   D. They invest customers' savings in the stock market.

7. _____ are financial institutions that serve people with a common concern, workplace, or community.

   A. Savings banks

   B. Community agencies

   C. Commercial banks

   D. Credit unions

8. What does 'payable on demand' mean with regard to checking accounts?

   A. A bank must exchange a signed check for cash upon receipt.

   B. A bank can demand cash in exchange for a signed check.

   C. A bank can hold a check for one week upon receipt.

   D. A check does not have to be signed in order to be cashed.

Personal Banking

In addition to keeping your money safe, banks also offer other services. Some of these services require a fee.

Directions: Read the questions below. Then select the best answers.

9. If you have a personal checking account, you can

    A. pay bills late.

    B. earn a huge amount of interest.

    C. have someone write a check using your name.

    D. withdraw money by writing a check or using an ATM.

10. When you write a check for more than the balance in your checking account, the bank will probably

    A. forgive you, if it is the first time.

    B. close your account temporarily.

    C. charge you a penalty fee.

    D. hold the check until you have enough money in the account.

11. Every reputable bank is required to

    A. protect customer privacy.

    B. offer savings incentives.

    C. offer free checking.

    D. publicize consumer account information.

12. When you withdraw money from a bank, a form of identification is required. What is the rationale behind this policy?

    A. It keeps a person's money safe.

    B. It allows the tracking of personal spending.

    C. It eases the transfer of funds.

    D. It prevents someone from loaning money.

13. Why do banks keep some money in reserve?

    A. They need to keep interest-earning accounts for savers.

    B. They want to have money set aside for large commercial loans.

    C. They need to have money set aside to cover future withdrawals.

    D. They want to earn interest on the money in customers' checking accounts.

Directions: Use the graphic below to answer questions 14–16.

[Check image showing check number 1936, with PAY TO THE ORDER OF, DATE, $, DOLLARS, FOR fields, and routing numbers ⑆000000186⑆ 000000529⑉ 1000]

14. On December 12, 2014, Clara Partridge needs to write a check to the Leadville Water Co. in the amount of $153.23. What information should appear in the white box on the check?

   A. 1936

   B. 152.23

   C. Clara Partridge

   D. December 12, 2014

15. The previous check written from this account was number _____.

   A. 1934

   B. 1935

   C. 1937

   D. 1938

16. What information must be added to the back of this check for it to be cashed?

   A. the account holder's address

   B. the recipient's signature

   C. the recipient's account number

   D. the account holder's signature

Directions: On a separate sheet of paper, write a response to the following question.

17. During a financial crisis in 2008, borrowers were not able to repay loans and many lending companies were going out of business. Lending, which stimulates the economy, slowed greatly. The national government and the Fed loaned money to financial institutions and banks on the verge of collapse. Some people felt this was necessary in order to avoid a collapse of the entire financial system. Others believe a collapse was not eminent and the government should not have bailed out the financial institutions. Do you agree or disagree with the actions of the government and the Fed? Explain your opinion.

Test-Taking Tip

How much should you write on a writing test? The answer is—as much as you feel is necessary to clearly answer the question and to provide supporting evidence. If you do not have much to say about the topic, do not try to stretch your material. Adding extraneous or irrelevant information just to add more length can harm your overall score.

Types of Consumer Credit Lesson 8.2

This lesson will help you identify several basic types of consumer credit, compare the different types of consumer credit, and describe situations in which each type of credit is useful. Use it with core lesson 8.2 Types of Consumer Credit to reinforce and apply your knowledge.

Key Concept
Different types of credit have different purposes and different advantages and disadvantages.

Core Skills & Practices
- Sequence Events
- Judge the Relevance of Information

Credit

Credit allows you to own something you want or need and to pay for it later. It is a convenient way to purchase and a threat to lower your ability to purchase what you might need in the future.

Directions: Read the questions below. Then select the best answers.

1. How do credit card companies such as banks earn most of their money?

    A. by charging consumers interest and fees on their debts

    B. by adding a few percentage points to the cost of items sold

    C. by charging participating retail outlets 5 percent on each sale

    D. by selling their credit cards to consumers

2. Complete the chart below by filling in the missing information that describes credit cards, installment loans, and secured loans.

home equity loan	small purchases	paid over a specific period of time

lowest interest rate	highest interest rate

Credit card		
Installment loan	new car	
Secured loan		lowest interest rate

2014 GED® Test Exercise Book

Directions: Answer the following question.

3. Secured-loan interest rates are usually low because

   A. the lenders have more money.

   B. the lenders assume very little risk.

   C. the borrowers have higher credit ratings.

   D. the loan is for a short period of time.

Directions: Use one of the terms below to complete the statement in question 4.

| credit report | credit score | bank statement |

4. A _____ is a report by a credit agency of how consistently you pay your bills.

Directions: Use the chart below to answer questions 5 and 6.

Year	Credit Score
2009	560
2010	620
2011	500
2012	540

5. The chart above details the changes in Mr. Fernandez's credit score from 2009-2012. Between 2010 and 2011, Mr. Fernandez most likely

   A. earned more money.

   B. obtained a low-interest credit card.

   C. purchased a new home.

   D. missed credit card payments.

6. The credit agency that issued these scores most likely obtained its information from

   A. employers and retail stores.

   B. the Internal Revenue Service and employers.

   C. banks and credit card companies.

   D. financial institutions and Social Security records.

Directions: Read the question below. Then select the best answer.

7. A home equity loan is a secured loan that might help reduce your taxes if

   A. your credit score is high.

   B. the interest is tax deductible.

   C. it is used to purchase a car.

   D. you pay a lot in interest.

Comparing Types of Credit

Different types of credit have different advantages and disadvantages.

Directions: Use the chart below to answer question 8.

8. Place the following events in chronological order:
   - Harriet's credit score drops.
   - A lender refuses to finance Harriet's used car purchase.
   - Harriet misses two credit card payment dates.
   - Harriet gets her first credit card.
   - Harriet gradually builds up her credit card balance.

1
2
3
4
5

✓ Test-Taking Tip

When a test requires you to put steps or items in a cause-and-effect sequence, it is sometimes helpful to work backwards. Find the last item or the final result. Then work backwards from there. Find the item that caused the final result. Continue until you have all the items placed in order. Then look at the items from the first item to the last to make sure that each item would cause the next item to happen.

Directions: Read the questions below. Then choose the correct answers.

9. An installment loan to buy a home is a good idea if a person has a down payment and

   A. interest rates are high.

   B. the property value is declining.

   C. the home is a large one.

   D. the buyer has a reliable source of income.

10. Legally, you have a right to look at your credit report once each

    A. year

    B. month

    C. week

    D. day

Directions: Read the passage below. Then answer questions 11 and 12.

> A recent study done by two professors at The Ohio State University indicates that younger people are more at risk from credit card debt. For example, a person born between 1980 and 1984 has debt higher than the previous two generations—$5,689 higher than their parents and $8,156 higher than their grandparents.
>
> "Our projections are that the typical credit card holder among younger Americans who keeps a balance will die still in debt to credit card companies."

11. Total credit card debt in the United States is a detriment to our economic future. This is a serious concern because research shows that

    A. the problem seems to be getting worse with each generation.

    B. few people are paying down their credit card debt before they die.

    C. credit card interest continues to rise.

    D. credit card companies will be less likely to lend to younger people.

Directions: Use one of the terms below to complete the statement in question 12.

mortgages	loans	credit reports	balances

12. One way future credit cardholders can break this pattern is by paying off their _____ each month.

108   Chapter 8 | Lesson 8.2 | Types of Consumer Credit

Consumer Credit Laws Lesson 8.3

This lesson will help you understand the importance of consumer credit laws such as the Equal Credit Opportunity Act, the Consumer Credit Protection Act, and the Truth in Lending Act. Use it with core lesson 8.3 Consumer Credit Laws to reinforce and apply your knowledge.

Key Concept
The federal government enforces laws that provide many safeguards for the consumer using credit.

Core Skills & Practices
- Analyze Point of View
- Identify Author's Bias

Consumer Credit Protections

Since the 1960s, the federal government has passed a variety of consumer credit protection laws to prevent discrimination, to ensure that consumers have clear information about the terms of credit, and to limit fees and interest rates that lenders can charge.

Directions: Read the passage below. Then answer the questions that follow.

> If . . . the consumer requests a copy of a consumer report from the person who procured the report, then, within 3 business days of receiving the consumer's request, together with proper identification, the person must send or provide to the consumer a copy of a report and a copy of the consumer's rights as prescribed by the Bureau. . .
>
> A consumer may elect to have the consumer's name and address excluded from any list provided by a consumer reporting agency under subsection (c)(1)(B) in connection with a credit or insurance transaction that is not initiated by the consumer, by notifying the agency in accordance with paragraph (2).
>
> —The Fair Credit Reporting Act

1. The Fair Credit Reporting Act and its amendments include several provisions such as

   A. allowing consumers access to their credit reports.

   B. protections against exceeding a credit limit.

   C. protection from discrimination on the basis of race, sex, or religion.

   D. the right to a free credit report each month.

2. The "Opt Out" provision of the Fair Credit Reporting Act says that a consumer may choose to have

   A. his or her name removed from lender marketing lists.

   B. his or her name removed from lists shared by a consumer reporting agency.

   C. personal information removed from the credit reporting agency files.

   D. no credit card business transactions collected by credit reporting agencies.

Directions: Read the following questions. Then select the correct answers.

3. The Truth in Lending Act limits a consumer's _____, or legal responsibility, for purchases if a credit card is stolen and used by someone else.

   A. liability
   B. credit report
   C. Credit CARD Act
   D. Equal Credit Opportunity Act

4. The _____ prohibits discrimination in credit transactions based on race, religion, sex, national origin, age, or marital or economic status.

   A. liability
   B. credit report
   C. Credit CARD Act
   D. Equal Credit Opportunity Act

Directions: Read the passage below. Then answer the questions that follow.

> Dear Editor:
>
> The federal government has tried to protect credit cardholders for years. But problems persist. For example, retailers continue to approve "over the limit" purchases that often result in huge fees from the credit card companies. These companies impose a retroactive interest rate of 25 to 30 percent if a cardholder is one day late! They advertise "No Interest for 6 Months" and then charge huge interest if the balance isn't then paid in full. How is a person supposed to get out of debt if penalty rates are 40 percent? We need new legislation to prevent these companies from misleading the public.
>
> Sincerely,
> J.Q Public

5. The writer believes which of the following has been ineffective?

   A. The Fair Credit and Charge Card Disclosure Act
   B. The Truth in Lending Act
   C. The Credit CARD Act
   D. Consumer Financial Protection Bureau

6. The writer believes that federal credit card protection has been

   A. inadequate to deal with the problems facing cardholders.
   B. too tough on credit card companies.
   C. able to deal with all but a few cardholder problems.
   D. unenforced since the early 1960s.

 Test-Taking Tip

When completing multiple-choice questions, don't keep changing your answer. If you are not sure, your first instinct is usually right, unless you misread the question.

Recent Credit Protections

The federal government expanded credit protections in the 1980s and 2000s.

Directions: Read the checklist below. Then answer the questions that follow.

Checklist for Credit Card Applicants

☐ What are the annual percentage rates (APRs)?
- for purchases?
- for cash advances?
- for balance transfers?
- if you pay late?

☐ What type of interest does the card have?

☐ How long is the grace period (the number of days you have to pay your bill in full without triggering a finance charge)?
- if you carry over a balance?
- if you pay the balance each month?
- for cash advances?

☐ How is the finance charge calculated?

☐ What are the fees?
- annual
- late payment
- setup
- over the credit limit

☐ What are the cash advance features?

☐ How much is the credit limit?

☐ Does the card offer other features?
- rebates
- insurance
- frequent-flyer miles

---

7. You would expect that for most credit cards the lowest APRs would be on

   A. frequent-flyer miles

   B. loans

   C. interest

   D. purchases

8. Credit card providers are prohibited from offering

   A. rebates.

   B. no-interest loans.

   C. insurance.

   D. frequent-flyer miles.

9. Which of these is the most basic question that a prospective credit card owner should know?

   A. "What are the cash advance features?"

   B. "What is the APR for purchases?"

   C. "Are there frequent-flyer miles?"

   D. "How much is the over-the-credit-limit fee?"

10. First-time credit card users should be interested in the credit _____ of the card.

    A. limit

    B. experience

    C. report

    D. advance

Directions: Use the chart below to answer questions 11–12.

Credit Card Information

New balance	$3,000.00
Minimum payment due	$90.00
Payment due date	4/20/12

Late Payment Warning: If we do not receive your minimum payment by the date listed above, you may have to pay a $35 late fee and your APRs may be increased up to the Penalty APR of 28.99%.

Minimum Payment Warning: If you make only the minimum payment each period, you will pay more in interest and it will take you longer to pay off your balance. For example:

If you make no additional charges using this card and each month you pay...	You will pay off the balance shown on this statement in about...	And you will end up paying an estimated total of...
Only the minimum payment	11 years	$4,745
$103	3 years	$3,712 (Savings = $1,033)

11. Based on current federal protections, you can predict that this consumer's next payment due date will most likely be

    A. 5/1/12.

    B. 5/20/12.

    C. 5/31/12.

    D. 4/20/13.

12. These protections were put into place by the

    A. Truth in Lending Act.

    B. Consumer Credit Protection Act.

    C. Equal Credit Opportunity Act.

    D. Credit CARD Act.

Development of Ancient Civilizations Lesson 9.1

This lesson will help you understand the development of ancient North Africa and the Indian Subcontinent, early Chinese civilization, and ancient Greece and Rome. Use it with core lesson 9.1 Development of Ancient Civilizations to reinforce and apply your knowledge.

Key Concept

Ancient civilizations shared the same six developments: cities, central government, religion, social and economic classes, art and architecture, and writing.

Core Skills & Practices

- Draw Evidence from Text
- Understand Cause and Effect

Ancient North Africa and the Indian Subcontinent

Ancient civilizations sprang up in North Africa along the banks of the Nile River and on the Indian subcontinent along the banks of the Indus and Ganges rivers.

Directions: Use the map below to answer questions 1–4.

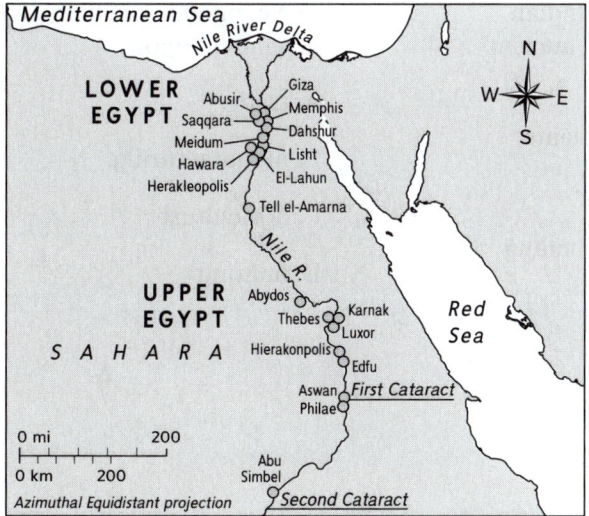

1. As shown in the map above, the Nile River became the center of a sophisticated Egyptian _____, or a society in an advanced state of cultural development.

   A. transportation

   B. colony

   C. river delta

   D. civilization

2. Ancient Egypt is sometimes called the "gift of the Nile," because

   A. Egypt depended on the Nile for transportation.

   B. the Nile's annual floodwater made agriculture possible.

   C. it is the world's longest river.

   D. fishing was one of Egypt's largest industries.

3. Egyptians built the pyramids

   A. near the Nile delta.

   B. on the shores of the Red Sea.

   C. to house government documents.

   D. to defend against invasion.

4. The pharaoh _____ was buried in the Great Pyramid of Giza.

   A. Ra

   B. Menes

   C. Khufu

   D. Osiris

Directions: Read the passage below. Then answer the questions that follow.

> The earliest civilization on the Indian subcontinent began in the Indus River Valley, dating back to around 2500 B.C. to 1500 B.C. Much of what we know is based on archaeological research from two cities, Harappa and Mohenjo-Daro. The two cities both were laid out on a grid pattern. Houses had running water and indoor plumbing that drained into a citywide sewage system. A combined temple, palace, and fort stood over each city on a nearby hill. Both cities had villages and fields scattered around them and large warehouses where crops were stored.

5. What did early civilizations on the Indian subcontinent have in common with ancient Egyptian civilization?

   A. Both built large religious monuments.

   B. Both began around 2500 B.C.

   C. Both had indoor plumbing and running water.

   D. Both were centered near rivers.

6. The economies of both civilizations were dependent upon

   A. trade.

   B. manufacturing.

   C. agriculture.

   D. hunting.

Early Chinese Civilizations

Chinese civilization was based on dynasties, and family was important to the structure of Chinese society.

Directions: Read the passage below. Then answer the questions that follow.

The Mandate of Heaven

To understand almost every aspect of Chinese culture, one must understand the concept of the Mandate of Heaven. It explains the dynastic cycles in China over the centuries beginning around the 11th century B.C.

The Duke of Zhou, younger brother of King Wu of the Western Zhou dynasty, first explained the Mandate of Heaven's four principles: 1. The right to rule is granted by Heaven. 2. There is one Heaven, therefore only one ruler. 3. The right to rule depends on the virtue of the ruler. 4. The right to rule is not limited to one dynasty. In other words, a ruler may lose the Mandate of Heaven. The Zhou dynasty explained its overthrow of the Shang dynasty based on the Mandate.

7. The term *mandate* most likely means

   A. an orange

   B. a command

   C. the title of the ruler

   D. the language they spoke

8. The Mandate of Heaven was used to explain the overthrow of

   A. Chinese dynasties beginning in the 11th century B.C.

   B. the Shang dynasty by the Zhou.

   C. King Wu of the Western Zhou.

   D. all governments in Asian countries.

9. Unlike the ruling philosophy of the Egyptians, the Mandate of Heaven

   A. says that the ruler can lose the right to rule.

   B. presents the ruler as a divine figure.

   C. teaches that the ruler is Heaven's choice.

   D. Attempted to preserve and stabilize the government.

Directions: Use the chart below to answer question 10.

10. Sort each of these terms into the ancient civilizations column with which they are associated.

    | Mandate of Heaven | papyrus | citywide sewage system |

Egyptian	
Chinese	
Indus River Valley	

2014 GED® Test Exercise Book

Ancient Greece and Rome

The ancient civilizations of Greece and Rome were located in the Mediterranean region. Like other ancient civilizations, they also developed in river valleys.

Directions: Read the passage below. Then answer the questions that follow.

> In 509 B.C., the Romans overthrew the Etruscan king and set up a republic. In a republic, citizens elect representatives to govern. This is different from the democracy that Athens developed, where citizens govern directly through voting. In Rome, wealthy landowners called patricians initially made most decisions regarding who would govern. Small landowners, farmers, craft workers, and merchants, known as plebeians, had little say. The government was headed by two **consuls**. The consuls issued laws and orders and could veto each other's decisions. A senate made sure that the laws and orders of the consuls were carried out, and it advised the consuls on issues. In time, the plebeians gained a larger voice in Roman government. By 409 B.C., plebeians had gained the right to hold public office. After 287 B.C., the Assembly of the People, which included all male citizens, could make laws that all Romans had to obey.

11. Which of the following best explains the difference between the governments of ancient Egypt and China with those of ancient Greece and Rome?

    A. The governments of Greece and Rome did not recognize a class system.

    B. The governments of Greece and Rome were not based on agriculture.

    C. The governments of Greece and Rome allowed ordinary citizens to participate.

    D. The governments of Greece and Rome had no official rulers.

12. The government of ancient Greece was different from that of ancient Rome in that

    A. Roman citizens did not directly participate in government.

    B. Roman citizens were not allowed to vote on laws.

    C. Roman citizens had to own land to participate in government.

    D. Roman citizens could veto the actions of the Senate.

Nationhood and Statehood Lesson 9.2

This lesson will help you understand boundaries and borders, why borders often follow natural features, and how cooperation and conflict influence the division of Earth's surface. Use it with core lesson 9.2 Nationhood and Statehood to reinforce and apply your knowledge.

Key Concept	Core Skills & Practices
Political and geographic boundaries divide the Earth into different regions and nations.	• Synthesize Ideas from Multiple Sources • Analyze Author's Purpose

Boundaries and Borders

Boundaries are lines that separate one area of Earth from another area.

Directions: Use the map below to answer questions 1 and 2.

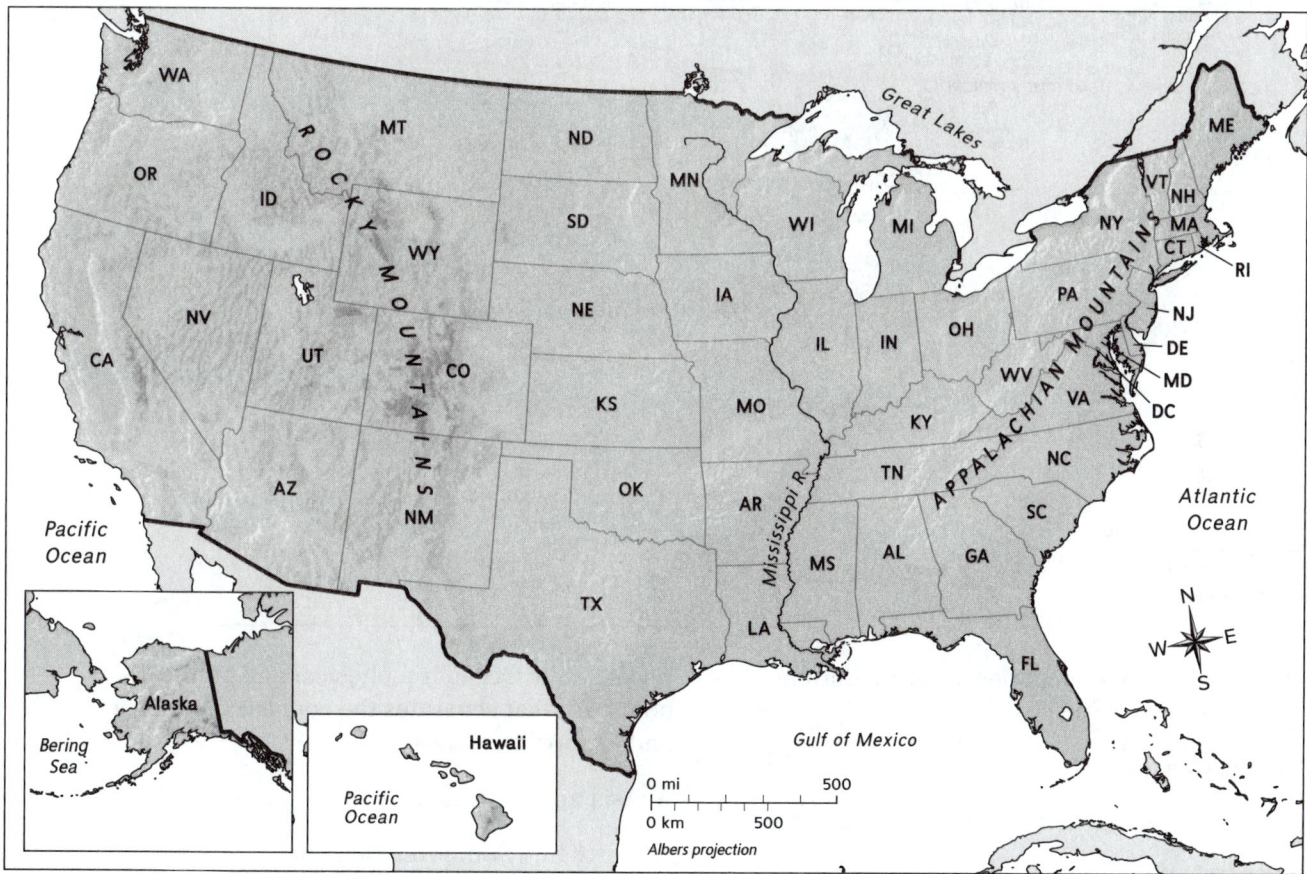

1. The Pacific Ocean serves is a border for _____ states.

   A. three

   B. four

   C. five

   D. six

2. The _____ of ten states coincide with the Mississippi River.

   A. borders

   B. rivers

   C. mountains

   D. state lines

2014 GED® Test Exercise Book

Directions: Use the map below to answer questions 3 and 4.

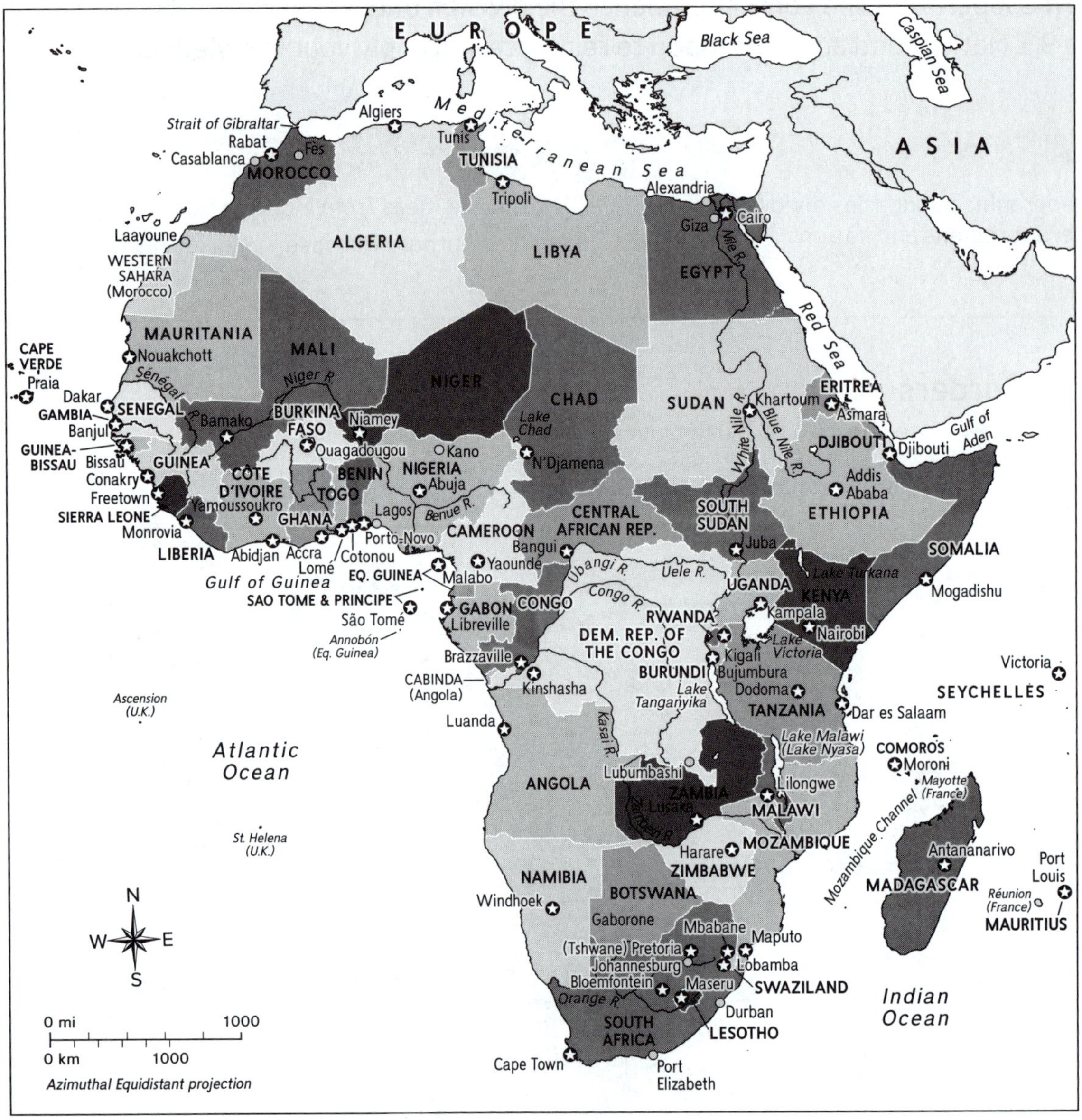

3. Which two physical boundaries separate Europe and Asia and from Africa?

   A. Atlantic Ocean and Indian Ocean

   B. Mediterranean Sea and Red Sea

   C. Mozambique Channel and Indian Ocean

   D. Nile River and Mediterranean Sea

4. The Atlantic Ocean is a physical and political boundary that separates the countries in Africa and Europe from those in

   A. Asia and Australia.

   B. North and South America.

   C. North America and East Asia.

   D. Antarctica.

✓ Test-Taking Tip

When taking a test, you may see an image that goes with a question. Read the question first to determine exactly what it is asking. Then look at the image with the purpose of gathering only the details that will help you answer the question.

Geometric Borders

Some borders that follow imaginary lines such as lines of longitude and latitude are called geometric borders.

Directions: Use the map below to answer question 5.

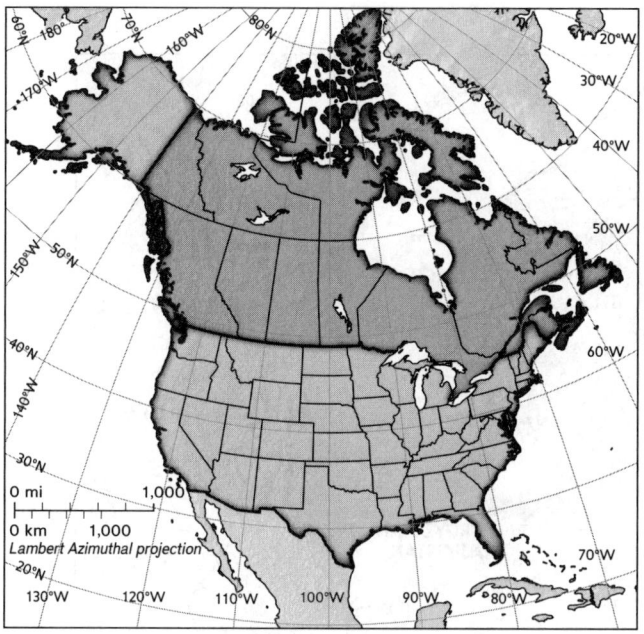

5. The degrees of lines of longitude increase from

   A. north to south.

   B. south to north.

   C. east to west.

   D. west to east.

Directions: Use the words **latitude** or **longitude** to fill in the blanks to questions 7 through 9.

6. Lines of _____ are not "parallels" because they meet at the poles.

7. The Equator is a line of _____.

8. The Prime Meridian is a line of _____.

9. Lines of latitude increase in value

   A. from north to south.

   B. from south to north.

   C. further from the equator.

   D. closer to the equator.

10. Latitude and longitude are measured in

    A. kilometers.

    B. miles.

    C. degrees.

    D. angles.

The Creation of Borders

People create borders separating ethnic and national groups sometimes through war and sometimes through negotiations.

Directions: Use the maps below to answer questions 11–13.

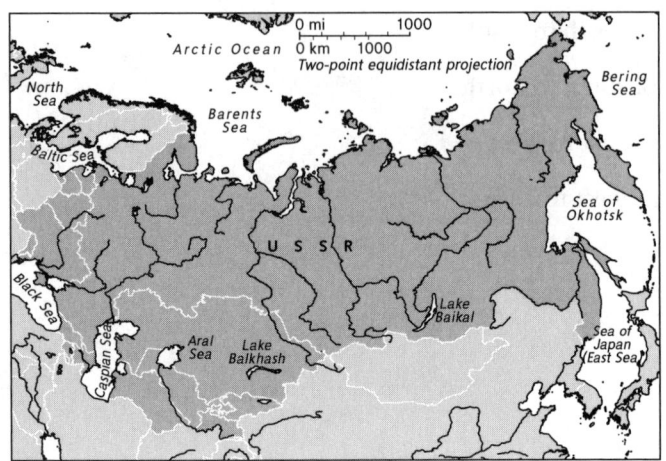

11. The two maps above illustrate changing borders as a result of

    A. World Wars I and II.

    B. the Russian Revolution and the breakup of the Soviet Union in 1991.

    C. an alliance between Russia and its neighbors that still exists today.

    D. negotiations that the United Nations conducted in the 1990s.

12. The fact that Kazakhstan has separate boundaries in the second map indicates that it has become a(n)

    A. independent nation.

    B. colony.

    C. isolated region.

    D. physical boundary.

13. Because the dissolution of the Soviet Union occurred without a war, these new boundaries were most likely created using

    A. force.

    B. conflict.

    C. longitude.

    D. cooperation.

Human Activity and the Environment Lesson 9.3

This lesson will help you discuss the effects of population growth and economic development, explain carrying capacity and global warming, and define sustainability and give examples of sustainable development. Use it with core lesson 9.3 Human Activity and the Environment to reinforce and apply your knowledge.

Key Concept
Economic development and a growing population are affecting the environment on Earth. Many people want to enact new policies to preserve Earth's natural resources.

Core Skills & Practices
- Draw Evidence from Text
- Analyze Ideas

Population Growth and Economic Development

As Earth's population continues to rise, and as more and more of its natural resources are being used, many people are concerned about how these changes will affect our environment.

Directions: Use the passage below to answer questions 1 and 2.

> Since taking office, I have supported an all-of-the-above energy approach that will allow us to take control of our energy future, one where we safely and responsibly develop America's many energy resources—including natural gas, wind, solar, oil, clean coal, and biofuels—while investing in clean energy and increasing fuel efficiency standards to reduce our dependence on foreign oil.
>
> … I have made the largest investment in clean energy and energy efficiency in American history and proposed an ambitious Clean Energy Standard to generate 80 percent of our electricity from clean energy sources like wind, solar, clean coal, and natural gas by 2035.
>
> —President Barack Obama

1. President Obama's main concern seems to be developing more energy sources that are

   A. nonrenewable.
   B. profitable.
   C. renewable.
   D. expensive.

2. Which of the following best explains why President Obama would take an "all-of-the-above" approach to finding energy sources?

   A. Without new sources, the United States might exceed its carrying capacity.
   B. The president needs to be careful not to alienate any voting group.
   C. The United States does not have enough of any one particular source of energy.
   D. Some citizens refuse to use certain types of energy sources.

 Test-Taking Tip

Some test items ask about specific words or phrases, paragraphs, or sections of a passage. Before answering a question about a text detail, reread the related sentence or paragraph whether or not the item directs you to reread it. As you reread, focus on what the question is about. For example, if the item is about the meaning of a word, think about how the word is used as you reread.

Directions: Read the following questions. Then select the correct answer.

3. Resources such as oil are _____ because they cannot be replaced in a short time.

   A. renewable

   B. fossil fuels

   C. natural resources

   D. nonrenewable

4. Which of the following would have the greatest impact in reducing greenhouse gas emissions in the United States?

   A. reducing electricity use

   B. increasing transportation use

   C. reducing amount of agriculture

   D. increasing the amount of agriculture

Global Warming and Climate Change

Carbon dioxide is one of many gases that cause Earth's greenhouse effect, or its ability to prevent some heat from the sun from escaping back into space. Without the greenhouse effect, Earth would be too cold for life.

Directions: Use the passage below to answer questions 5 and 6.

> Francisco Estrada is an ecological economist at the Free University in Amsterdam. He studied temperature data from 1850 to 2010 to determine if there was a correlation between fossil fuel emissions and global warming. Here is some of what he found:
>
> "A cooling period between 1940 and 1970 had previously been chalked up to natural variability and the Sun-shielding effect of pollution emitted by European industries, as they recovered after the Second World War. But Estrada and his colleagues found that it followed a reduction in greenhouse-gas emissions associated with economic downturns, when industries were less active. Significant drops in emissions occurred during the First World War, the Great Depression of the 1930s and the Second World War."
>
> —Hannah Hoag, *Nature*, November 10, 2013

5. What does Estrada now believe caused the cooling period between 1940 and 1970?

   A. a decrease in greenhouse gas emissions because of a decrease in the sun-shielding effect of pollution

   B. an increase in greenhouse gas emissions because of a decrease in the sun-shielding effect of pollution

   C. a decrease in greenhouse gas emissions because industries were less active

   D. an increase in greenhouse gas emissions because of the economic downturn

6. Why did greenhouse gas emissions drop during World War I, the Great Depression, and World War II?

   A. The economy was in an upswing.

   B. The sun-shield effect was stronger.

   C. Fewer fossil fuels were used.

   D. Industry was less active.

Sustainability

Sustainability is a term that refers to living within limits when it comes to the use of natural resources.

Directions: Read the following questions. Then select the correct answers.

7. As a response to a reduction in resources and an increase in the greenhouse effect, _____ development is economic development that uses natural resources without endangering supplies for the future.

   A. sustainable

   B. declining

   C. increasing

   D. industrial

8. In addition to the size and growth of Earth's human population, which of the following is a reason why Earth's natural resources are being depleted?

   A. Natural resources are becoming more costly to produce and distribute.

   B. Higher standards of living are allowing more people to use more resources.

   C. Decreased access to resources is leading to wasteful consumption.

   D. People are destroying resources to protest their unequal distribution.

Directions: Use the graph below to answer questions 9 and 10.

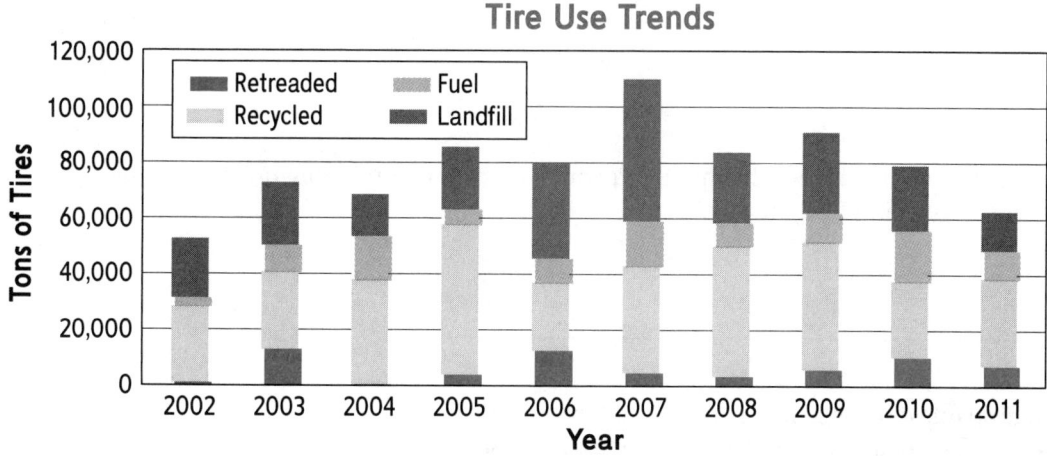

Source: http://www.ecy.wa.gov/programs/swfa/tires/reuse.html

9. How does the graph illustrate the concept of sustainable development?

   A. It shows that the amount of tires used as fuel has decreased.

   B. It shows that retreaded tires are the smallest portion of tires each year.

   C. It shows how many natural resources are being used to make new tires.

   D. It shows the amount of tires being reused and recycled.

10. Which year shows the most sustainability for tires?

    A. 2011

    B. 2007

    C. 2005

    D. 2003

2014 GED® Test Exercise Book

Directions: Read the following questions. Then select the best answer.

11. From the list of practices for sustainable development below, choose those that are the result of government policies and those that are individual and business decisions. Write each practice in the appropriate box.

    increasing gasoline taxes   recycling materials   walking to work
    limiting offshore oil drilling   turning out lights   subsidizing solar energy

Government Policies	
Individual and Business Decisions	

12. Automakers will produce smaller, more fuel-efficient automobiles when consumer _____ for them increases.

    A. care

    B. demand

    C. production

    D. GDP

13. On a separate sheet of paper, write a paragraph explaining which environmental issue you believe is most critical today. Provide reasoning for your choice.

Test-Taking Tip

When answering a drag-and-drop question, it is important to read the question carefully before selecting items. When you are sure you understand the question, carefully read the items to select. First, select the items you feel confident you know; then go back and work on the items about which you are less sure.

Concepts of Region and Place Lesson 10.1

This lesson will help you understand that natural resources are distributed and utilized in various ways, recognize the many ecosystems on Earth, and consider weather and climate systems. Use it with core lesson 10.1 Concepts of Region and Place to reinforce and apply your knowledge.

Key Concept

The planet Earth is made up of many interconnected physical systems, including land, water, plants, animals, and weather.

Core Skills & Practices

- Use Graphs
- Use Maps

Earth's Structure and Regions

The surface of the Earth is composed of vast oceans and large landmasses that have mountains, hills, valleys and plains.

Directions: Answer the following questions.

1. Place each of these landforms beside the proper descriptions below.

   | plain | plateau | isthmus | peninsula |

Landform	Description
	Strip of land surrounded by water on thee sides
	Large area of flat land, without trees
	Narrow strip of land between two land masses, water on each side
	Flat land that is raised above surrounding land surface

2014 GED® Test Exercise Book

Directions: Use the diagram below to answer questions 2–4.

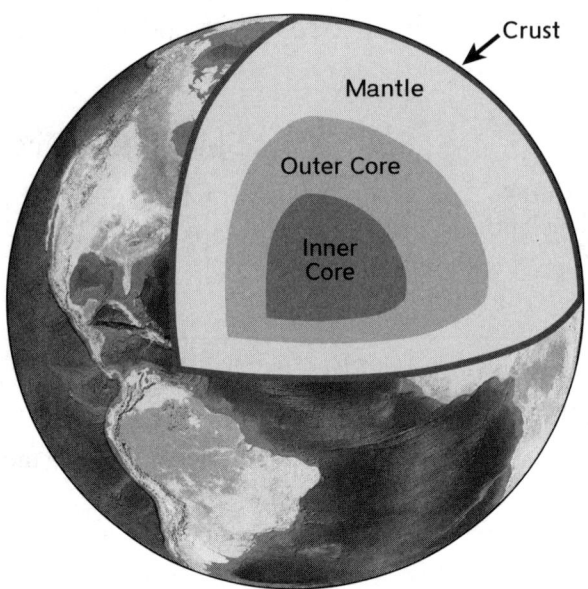

2. All living organisms on Earth live on the layer known as the

   A. crust.

   B. mantle.

   C. continent.

   D. ocean.

3. The difference between the outer and inner core can best be described as the difference between

   A. land and water.

   B. gas and solid.

   C. liquid and solid.

   D. heat and cold.

4. The thickest layer shown in this graphic is made of

   A. solid rock.

   B. liquid metal.

   C. hot gas.

   D. solid metal.

5. Soil, minerals, water, animals, and plants are _____ that are distributed unevenly across the Earth.

   A. fossil fuels

   B. Earth resources

   C. natural products

   D. natural resources

Directions: Use the graph below to answer questions 6 and 7.

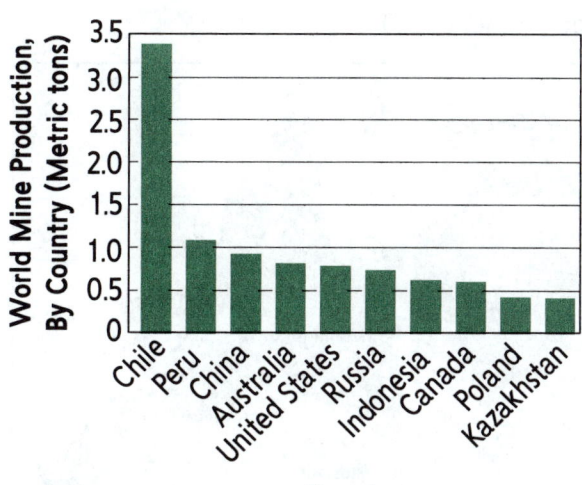

6. Chile produces more copper than

   A. the rest of the world combined.

   B. the next three highest producers combined.

   C. the next six highest producers combined.

   D. the world can use at this time.

7. Which two continents lead the world in copper production?

   A. Asia and Africa

   B. Australia and Europe

   C. North and South America

   D. Asia and Europe

Ecosystems

An ecosystem is a community of organisms in an area and the natural resources with which the community interacts.

Directions: Complete the chart below using the ecosystems provided.

8. Place the type of ecosystem in the box beside its organisms, natural resources, and climate.

grassland	forest	desert	lake

	Mosses, birds, wolves, fungi, squirrels
	Coyotes, hawks, bumblebees, rodents
	Iguana, kangaroo rat, prickly pear cactus, armadillo lizard
	Algae, reeds, duckweed, mollusks

Weather and Climate

Weather changes daily, but climate is determined by the weather patterns that an area experiences over a long period of time.

Directions: Use the map below to answer questions 9–10.

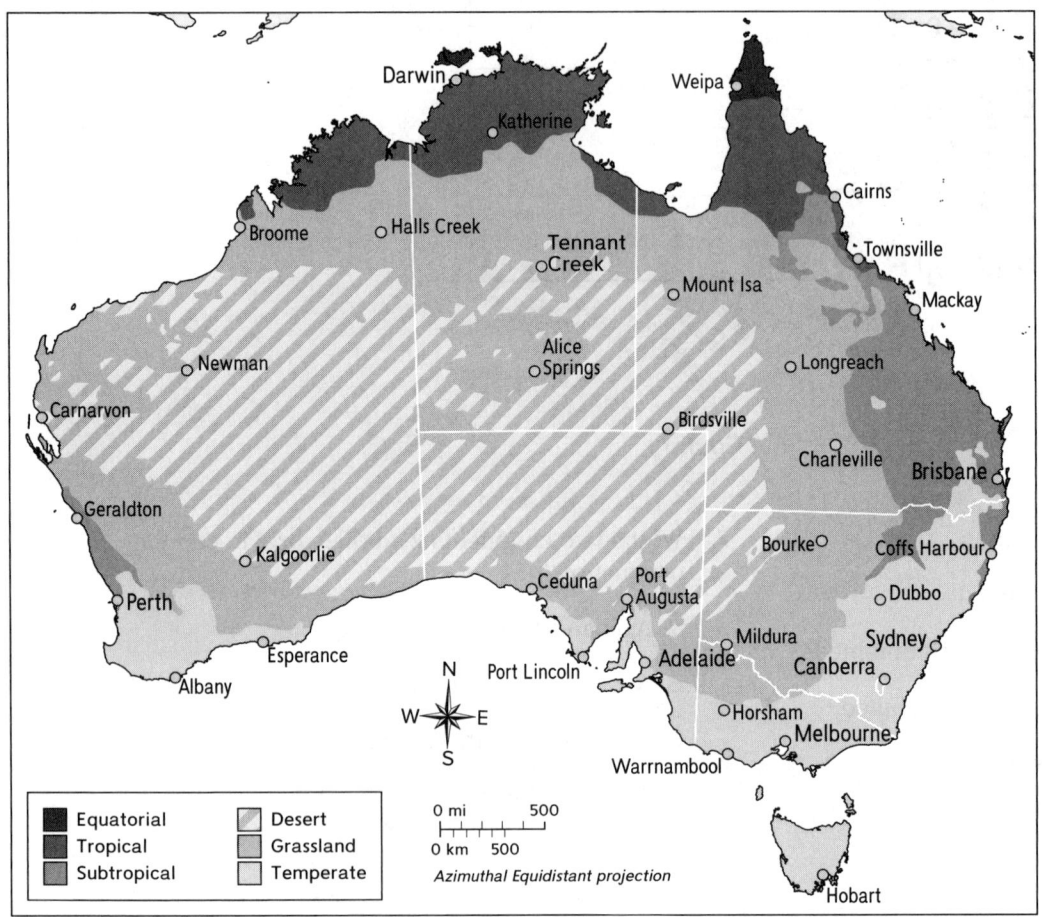

9. Because Australia is below the Equator, the tropical climate in the country is

   A. along the west coast.

   B. in the North.

   C. in the Southeast.

   D. very small.

10. Australia's large desert climate is

    A. more than 1600 kilometers wide.

    B. three-quarters the size of the entire country.

    C. surrounded by a subtropical climate.

    D. not fit for human habitation.

Natural and Cultural Diversity Lesson 10.2

This lesson will help you understand the diversity of physical and human geography and how landforms affect human settlement. Use it with core lesson 10.2 Natural and Cultural Diversity to reinforce and apply your knowledge.

Key Concept
Earth is rich in physical and cultural diversity, as seen by its landscapes and its people.

Core Skills & Practices
- Infer
- Evaluate Evidence

Physical Diversity

The landscapes of Earth exhibit vast diversity, from flat plains to rugged mountains and from wetlands and rivers to dry prairies and deserts.

Directions: Use the map below to answer questions 1 and 2.

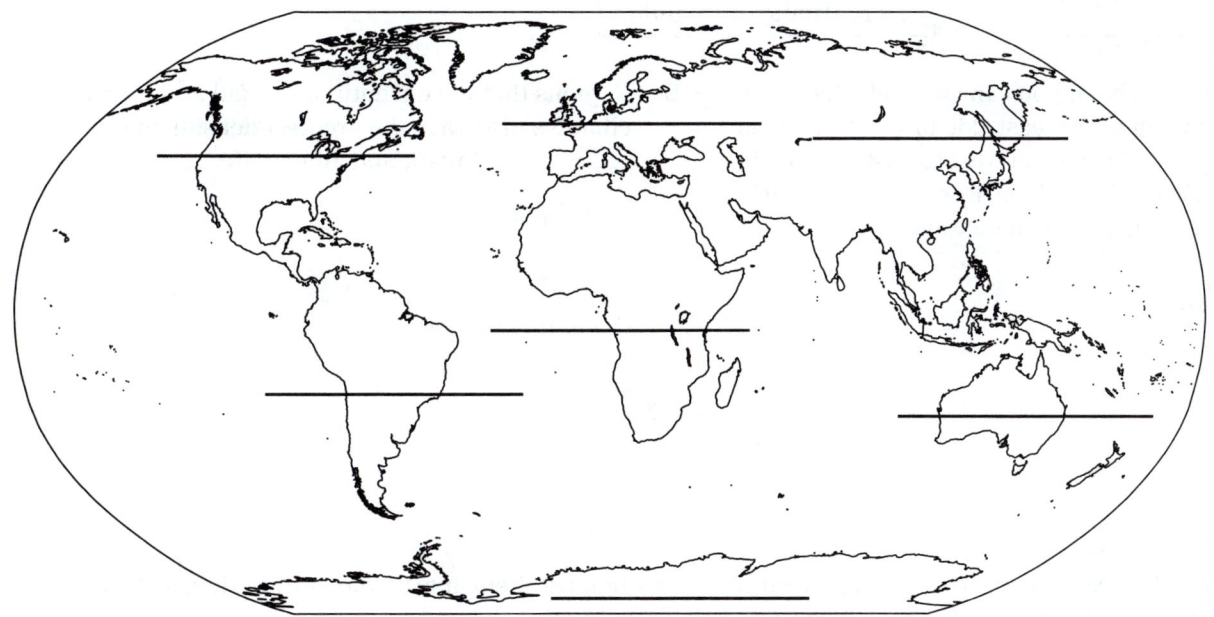

1. Write the names of each continent on the appropriate space on the map.

| South America | Asia | Europe | North America |

| Africa | Oceania | Antarctica |

2. Earth's five oceans are the Atlantic, Pacific,

   A. Indian, Mediterranean, and Arctic.

   B. Arctic, Arabian, and Northern.

   C. Southern, Arctic, and Indian.

   D. Mediterranean, Southern, and Indian.

2014 GED® Test Exercise Book   129

Directions: Use the chart below to answer questions 3–5.

Tropical wet	
Arid, desert	
Subarctic, tundra	
Humid continental	
Marine, West Coast	

3. Climate zones are determined by a region's characteristics such as latitude or distance from the Equator, nearness to a large body of water, air currents and landforms. Write each of the following descriptions next to the climate zone it describes in the chart above.

| interior Australia surrounded by mountains | near Equator and bordered by Pacific Ocean | interior region visited by storms and cloudy days |

| 60 degrees north latitude | frequent mild wet winds from Pacific or Atlantic |

4. Based on this chart, you can conclude that if you live in a valley on the east side of the mountains and the wind blows from west to east, it is likely that your rainfall would be less than that of the _____ side of the mountains.

   A. north
   B. south
   C. west
   D. east

5. Regions that have plenty of rainfall and warm climates also have the greatest density and _____ of plant and animal life.

   A. diversity
   B. quality
   C. characteristics
   D. quantity

Cultural Diversity

Just as Earth's physical regions have defining characteristics that set them apart from one another, so too do Earth's people have languages, customs, values, and beliefs that define them.

Directions: Read the following questions. Then select the correct answers.

6. If you were a visitor from another planet who encountered a human being, the human being would most likely speak

   A. English.
   B. Mandarin.
   C. Spanish.
   D. German.

7. Countries such as the United States and Nigeria that have many cultures within different regions are called

   A. American.
   B. multicultural.
   C. characteristic.
   D. ethnically similar.

Directions: Answer the following question.

8. There are more than 6,000 languages in the world. Many are closely related. Choose the members of the Indo-European language family, and drag them to the box below.

French **Japanese** **Sanskrit** **Greek**
Swahili **Mandarin** **Italian** **English**

Indo-European languages	

Directions: Use the chart below to answer questions 9 and 10.

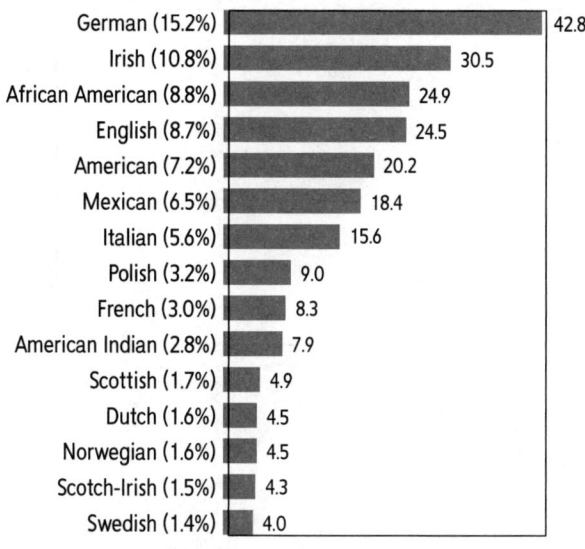

Source: U.S. Census Bureau, Census 2000 special tabulation.

9. The United States has a high number of German, Irish, African American, and English because

   A. more immigrants came from these areas.

   B. these groups tend to have more children than other groups.

   C. they tend to live longer than other groups.

   D. these groups came very early and have more descendants than other groups.

10. Why will this chart be less accurate over time?

    A. The Census Bureau is becoming less important.

    B. More people will have diverse, multicultural ancestries.

    C. The numbers will get too large to track.

    D. Some ethnic groups will stop growing.

Landforms and Human Settlement

Physical factors such as landforms, climate, and environment affect where people choose to settle and how their culture develops.

Directions: Read the following questions. Then select the correct answers..

11. The increasing movement of people and businesses into outlying areas around cities is often called

   A. emigration.

   B. urban sprawl.

   C. forced migration.

   D. suburban expansion.

12. Humans settle in certain regions, which affects how their societies develop. Study the cause-and-effect diagram below. Then drag the causes into the Causes box and the effects into the Effects box.

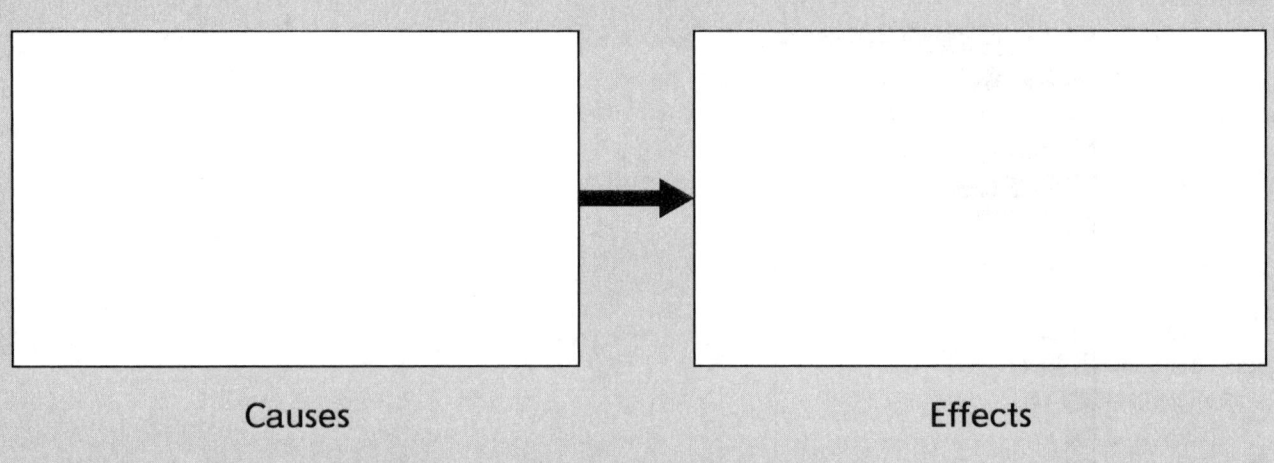

Causes   Effects

physical geography   clothing   climate
wildlife   language   building materials
culture   food   vegetation

 Test-Taking Tip

When answering a question related to a chart with a lot of data, read the question first so you can target the specific data in the chart needed to answer the question.

Population Trends and Issues Lesson 10.3

This lesson will help you understand what demography is; recognize that population growth and settlement patterns tell a great deal about how humans interact with their environment; and explain the general trend toward urban growth in the United States. Use it with core lesson 10.3 Population Trends and Issues to reinforce and apply your knowledge.

Key Concept
Humans interact with Earth by moving from place to place, building new communities, and expanding their populations.

Core Skills & Practices
- Analyze Information
- Display Data

Demography
The statistical study of the size, growth, movement, and distribution of people is called demography.

Directions: Use the map below to answer questions 1 and 2.

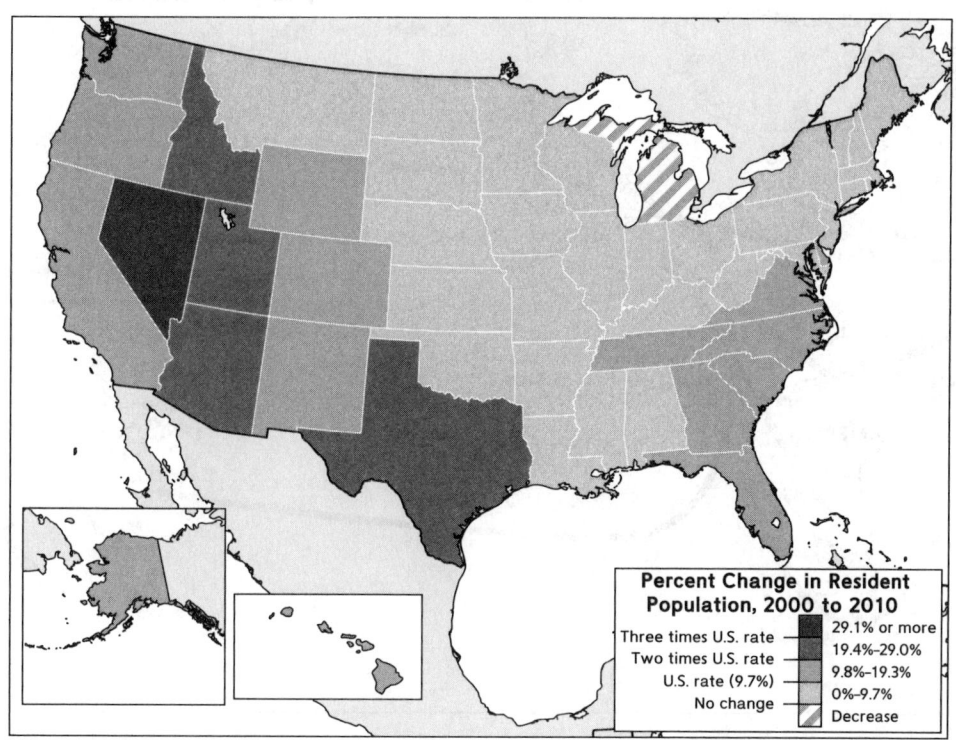

1. According to the information given in this graphic, in 2010, new government services might have been needed most in

   A. Virginia.

   B. Texas.

   C. Michigan.

   D. Nevada.

2. People were leaving which state and moving elsewhere?

   A. Michigan

   B. North Carolina

   C. Florida

   D. New York

Directions: Read the following questions. Then select the correct answers.

3. Demographic information includes a population's fertility rate and _____ rate, or death rate.

   A. growth
   B. decrease
   C. mortality
   D. increase

4. The main reason the government uses census data is to determine _____

   A. which states are the most successful.
   B. where new services might be needed.
   C. how much each person should be taxed.
   D. where citizens should move in the future.

Migration and Population

Migration, the movement of people from one place to another, can occur for a number of different reasons.

Directions: Use the map below to answer questions 5 and 6.

Eighteen Centuries of Migration

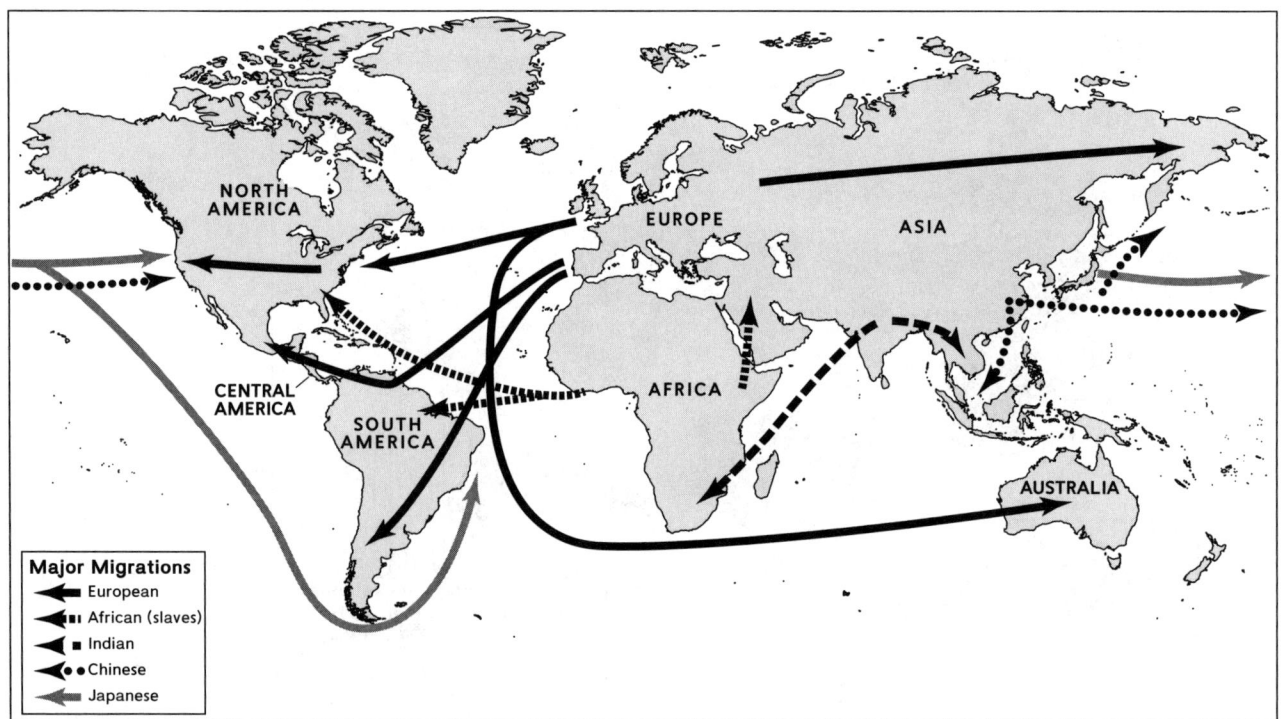

5. Wars, religious and political persecution, and food shortages caused the large migrations of which groups of people beginning in the 17th century?

   A. Africans
   B. Europeans
   C. Asians
   D. Chinese

6. In the late twentieth century, about 12 million people from the country of _____ and from Asia moved to the United States, largely because of persecution and poor economic conditions.

   A. Africa
   B. Europe
   C. Canada
   D. Mexico

Directions: Read the following questions. Then select the correct answers.

7. Which situation best indicates a growing population?

   A. low fertility and low mortality rates

   B. high fertility and low mortality rates

   C. low fertility and high mortality rates

   D. high fertility and high mortality rates

8. The term that describes the spreading of cultural traits from one part of the world to another is cultural _____.

   A. diversity

   B. diffusion

   C. growth

   D. quality

Urban Growth

The last two centuries witnessed a trend toward the movement of people from rural to urban areas.

Directions: Use the map below to answer questions 9 and 10.

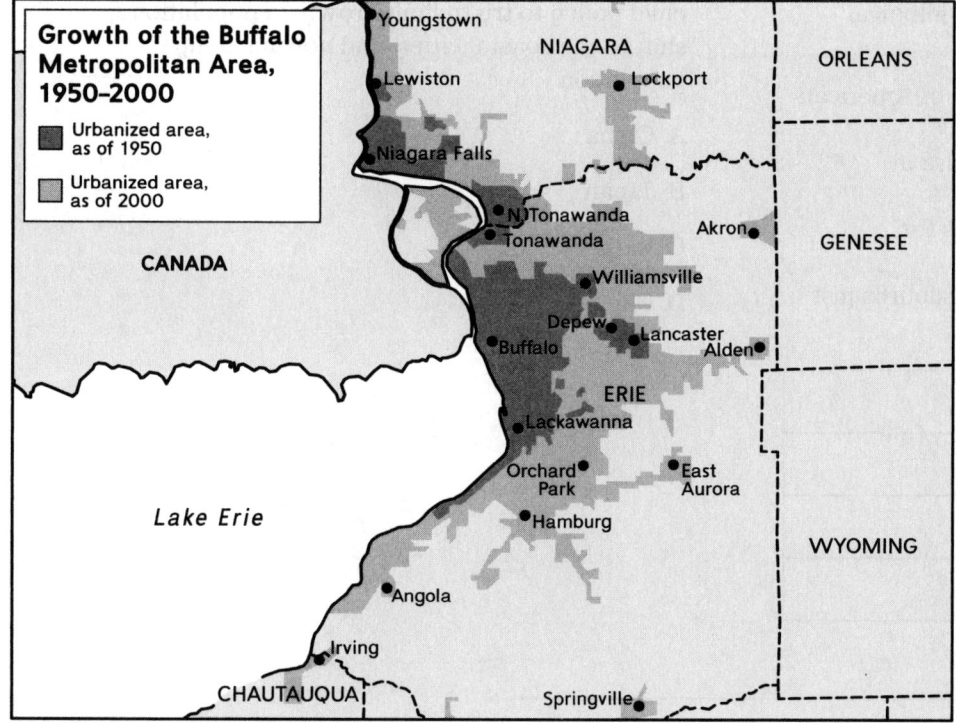

9. Buffalo, New York, may fit the description of "urban sprawl" because

   A. the city population declined and the metropolitan area expanded.
   B. more people today live near the center of the city.
   C. many farmers have moved from Niagara County to the city limits.
   D. the city continues to incorporate smaller towns into its governed area.

10. Which two counties have experienced significant population growth?

    A. Ontario and Wyoming
    B. Chatauqua and Orleans
    C. Erie and Niagara
    D. Lancaster and Orchard Park

Directions: Read the following questions. Then select the correct answers.

11. Based on what you know about urban migration, sequence these periods of population movement by writing the descriptions in chronological order.

    - Immigrants swell the population of American cities.
    - Urban sprawl creates communities in metropolitan areas.
    - People move from farms to cities for employment.
    - Many city dwellers move to the suburbs just outside the cities.

1800–1850	
1870–1950	
1950–1980	
1980–2010	

12. Over the last century, the nation of _____ has experienced huge population growth, a one-child policy to try to limit growth, a population shift to the coastal cities, and now an aging population.

    A. China
    B. Japan
    C. India
    D. Canada

Test-Taking Tip

You can understand a map by reading the title and looking at the map key to determine what information the map is conveying.

Answer Key

Lesson 1.1

1. **B** A monarchy is a type of government with a king or queen as head of state.
2. **C** The Magna Carta was written to protect English citizens from unjust treatment or punishment.
3. **A** The legislature in the United States and the parliament in Canada both contain representatives elected by citizens.
4. **D** Authoritarian governments do not protect the rights of individuals and are not based on popular sovereignty. Some still exist.
5. **C** Both Aristotle and Tocqueville are worried about the power of the poor versus the power of the rich. Aristotle says that government can be in the hands of the poor or in the hands of the wealthy, which can lead to continual disputes. Tocqueville says that Christian countries have "equality of conditions" now, but it is impossible to foresee how that might change in the future.
6. **B** Aristotle believes a democracy is like an oligarchy when the people in power are wealthy.
7. **D** Tocqueville is worried that citizens and capitalists will continue to be treated relatively equally in the future.
8. **A** Monarchs have ceremonial power, whereas dictators have absolute power.
9.

Author	Document
British nobles	Magna Carta
Thomas Jefferson	Declaration of Independence
George Mason	Virginia Declaration of Rights
Founders of US government	US Constitution

10.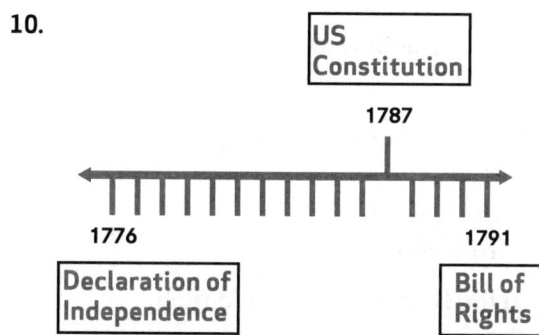

11. **C** The amendment process makes the Constitution a flexible document.
12. **B** The right to vote, regardless of color, was granted in the Fifteenth Amendment. Women's right to vote is granted in the Nineteenth Amendment.
13. **D** The right to vote for those eighteen years of age and older is granted in the Twenty-Sixth Amendment.
14. **C** Protecting the voting rights of citizens has been an ongoing process.
15. Student essay will vary, but should reflect an understanding of the limitations the framers of the Constitution placed on American government.

Answer Key

Lesson 1.2

1. **D** Natural rights are those given to the people by nature or God, and no government would have the right to violate them.

2. **B** A government based on a constitution holds only those powers granted in its written rules, known as its constitution.

3. Student essays will vary, but should present an adequate defense of their opinion and understanding of the Second Continental Congress.

4.

Shays's Rebellion, 1786–1787	
Cause	**Effect**
The Articles of Confederation did not make provisions for collecting taxes and paying off the nation's war debts. Each state had to collect its own taxes. Many farmers did not have enough money to pay their tax debts.	Courts and tax collectors seized farms as repayment for debt.
Several farmers in Massachusetts, including a Revolutionary War veteran named Daniel Shays, believed they were being treated unfairly and became angry.	The farmers took up arms against their state government.
The Articles of Confederation was seen as ineffective because it did not provide a strong central government.	The US Constitution was drafted and passed as a more effective plan of governing the people.

5. **C** Citizens hold the power, or popular sovereignty, in a government by electing their own representatives at all levels of government.

6. **C** The rule of law means that the law is preeminent over any other factor, including any leader, group, or concern.

7. **C** A faction is a smaller group of people who hold different views, which they make clear to the larger group.

8. **A** Madison believed that freedom (liberty) would not need to be limited, because the freedom exercised by many other groups would be enough to keep a faction from taking control.

9. **D** The colonists wanted to be sure that the rights that were violated by the British before and during the war—freedom of speech and the press, the right to bear arms, the right against illegal searches and seizures, for example—would be addressed in the new constitution.

10. **A** An amendment must be proposed by Congress and then ratified by a three-fourths majority of the states.

11. **A** Those with Asian ancestry were not large enough to make it into the graph, which includes only the top fifteen groups.

12. Because the Constitution can be amended, it will remain _____**relevant**_____ throughout time.

Lesson 1.3

1. **C** The president's chief job is to run the executive department.
2. **D** The president does not have the power to declare war; that responsibility belongs to the legislature.
3. **C** The judicial branch originally was supposed to hear only cases involving leaders of other nations or between states in the United States.
4. **C** The Supreme Court's original jurisdiction is to hear cases involving foreign leaders or between states.
5. **A** The first statement of the Presidential Oath of Office—"that I will faithfully execute the office of President"—defines his primary responsibility.
6. Because of the __media__, the president in the modern era can speak directly to the people, allowing his __case__ to be heard over the voices of Congress.
7. In the past, the __Congress__ had a more direct connection to the people as their representatives.
8. Answers will vary but should contain opinions supported with facts.
9.

Power	
To levy taxes Federal and State	To hold elections Federal and State
To enter into treaties with foreign countries Federal	To establish schools State
To set up local and county governments State	To borrow money Federal and State
To regulate trade within a state State	To declare war Federal

10. **B** The power to set up a bank is shared by both the state and federal government. This is known as a __concurrent__ power.
11. **D** Chief Justice Marshall said: "the power to tax involves the power to destroy." Marshall most likely meant that the __state__ governments could use that power to weaken the __federal__ government.
12. **chief executive** — heads his or her political group in the state

    party leader — denies or grants paroles, pardons, and reprieves

    judicial leader — sees that state laws are carried out, prepares an annual budget, appoints officials

    ceremonial leader — proposes, approves, or vetoes legislation

    chief legislator — is head of the National Guard of the state

    commander-in-chief — represents the state at functions, greets key visitors
13. **A** Citizens have the power to suggest legislation (direct initiative), to repeal legislation (referendum), and to vote an official out of office (recall).
14. **C** The lieutenant governor, like the vice president, presides over the legislature and replaces the governor if he dies, resigns, or is removed from office.

Answer Key

Lesson 2.1

1. **Civil Liberties:** gathering peacefully, voting, speaking your opinion; **Civil Rights:** attending school, living where you choose, employment
2. B Mason's ideas regarding due process were expressed in the Sixth Amendment.
3. B Along with the other protections it provides, due process prevents the government from conducting illegal searches.
4. C The right against self-incrimination described in this ruling is protected by the Fifth Amendment.
5. C The Thirteenth, Fourteenth, and Fifteenth Amendments guaranteed civil rights to African Americans.
6. C In 1896 the Supreme Court ruled that segregation was legal under the "separate but equal" doctrine.
7. C Dr. King's views are most clearly reflected in the Supreme Court's decision in *Brown v. Board of Education, Topeka, Kansas,* which declared segregation in public facilities unconstitutional.
8. B Sojourner Truth's famous speech argued that as a woman she was as strong and able as a man, proven by her strengths and experiences. She stood as an example of the strength of all women.
9. A Sojourner Truth showed that no man could outwork her because she had worked just as hard at planting and plowing and reaping as anyone.
10.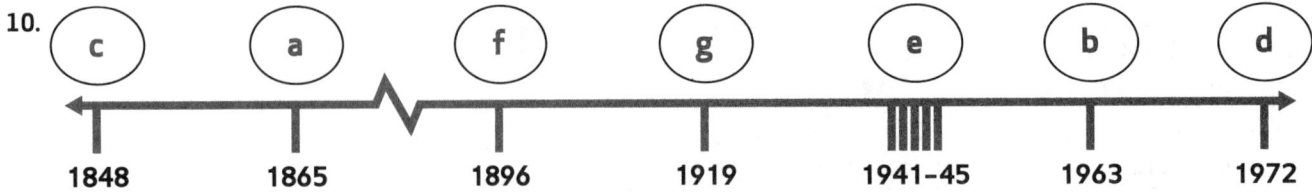
11. D It took tremendous perseverance to work hard for so long toward gaining civil rights for these groups.
12. B Title IX granted equal treatment to girls and women who play sports in school and/or college.
13. Answers will vary but should contain opinions supported by facts.

Lesson 2.2

1. C By identifying issues and concerns that were shared by different types of Americans, Senator Obama was most likely trying to appeal to independent voters.
2. A Senator Obama's speech helped outline his party's beliefs, a task that is one of a national convention's main goals.
3. C Third-party candidates often deal with an issue or a set of issues that some voters believe the major parties are not adequately addressing.
4. A Having a third-party candidate in a presidential election can sometimes effect the election of Republicans or Democrats running.
5. B Because the numbers of Democrats and Republicans are roughly the same, independents tend to tip the balance of an election in favor of the winning party.
6. B In American politics, an elephant is normally the symbol of the Republican Party.
7. C Political cartoons combine symbols and caricatures to convey a specific message.

8. **B** George W. Bush had won the most electoral votes. This won him the presidency, even though he lost the popular vote.

9. **D** Because they charge high fees for their services, lobbyists give wealthy individuals and groups a great deal of influence over the legislative process.

Lesson 2.3

1. **A** As it is used in this context, "domestic" refers to things that happen within one's own country.
2. **C** Posterity refers to the generations of people who will be US Citizens.
3.

Type of Policy	Type of government
Setting sanitation and waste collection standards	City
Defining military eligibility requirements	National
Enforcing local noise ordinances	City
Defining requirements for obtaining a driver's license	State
Adopting education standards and graduation requirements	State
Establishing trade practices with foreign countries	National

4.

Policy	Type of policy
Seatbelts must be worn by all passengers in a moving vehicle.	Public safety policy
Trucks cannot exceed posted weight limits on public highways.	Transportation policy
All vehicles must pass an emissions test before being issued a license plate.	Environmental policy
License plate renewal fees will be increased by 10% in the new year.	Economic policy
Drivers are required to carry medical liability coverage through their auto insurance carrier.	Healthcare policy

5. **A** While this statement reflects a personal preference or bias, all of the other statements can be proven or disproven with evidence.

6. Policy Implementation **4**

   Problem Identification **1**

   Policy Adoption **3**

   Policy Evaluation **5**

   Policy Formulation **2**

7. **C** Since the final step in the public policy process involves evaluating the effectiveness of the policy, public policy is always in the process of being reshaped and refined.

8. **D** The next step in the process after implementation of a policy is the evaluation of the results.

9. **B** Interest groups normally contribute to the process of policy formation.

Answer Key

10.

Special Interest Group	Public Interest Group	Economic Interest Group
Preventing Texting While Driving	Campaign Finance Reform	Improving Work Safety Standards
Gun Control	Increasing Voter Registration	Relaxing Health Care Regulations

11. A Lobbying is a process by which individuals and interest groups can influence the lawmaking process.

12. D According to this ruling, direct personal contact, such as buying lunch or dinner for government officials, can threaten the democratic process.

13. Student paragraphs will vary, but should contain well-supported ideas.

Lesson 3.1

1. C The Mayflower Compact was a written agreement that set out the rules by which the Pilgrims would govern themselves.

2. A Pennsylvania was settled by those seeking religious freedom.

3. B This document is an early example of a(n) charter.

4. C As used in this passage, a colony is a land controlled by another nation.

5. A Dickinson, like many colonists, opposed the Townshend Acts because they levied taxes on the colonists, who were not represented in the British Parliament.

6. D The colonists thought the taxes were unjust because they were not given representation in Parliament.

7. B Many colonists responded to the taxes mentioned in Dickinson's letter by participating in boycotts.

8. C The term indelibly means permanently.

9. B Since this passage asks the king to maintain peace and help his subjects—that is, the colonists—we can conclude that it is taken from the Olive Branch Petition.

10. D The Olive Branch Petition was an attempt at a truce following the Battles of Lexington and Concord.

11. C The king rejected the Olive Branch Petition.

12.

Articles of Confederation	Constitution
A. Passing laws requires approval of 9 of 13 states. E. Congress has no authority to pass taxes. F. Trade regulated by states	B. Government divided into three branches C. Representation based on population House of Representatives D. Each state gets one vote in Senate.

142

13.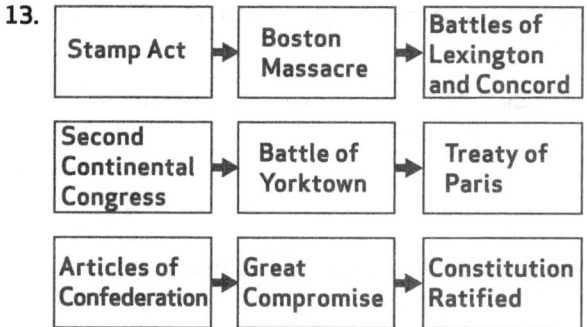

14. Student essays will differ, but should compare and contrast factual information.

Lesson 3.2

1. **D** The Northwest Ordinance of 1787 established the process by which new states could be added to the Union.

2. This document dealt with the organization of the western lands controlled by the United States; these lands are referred to as _____**territories**_____.

3. _____**Five**_____ states were added to the Union as a result of this document.

4. **C** All of these offices were originally appointed by President Washington.

5. **B** The State Department monitors conflicts among other nations.

6.

Treaty of Greenville	Treaty of Paris, 1783	Jay's Treaty	Pinckney's Treaty
B. Tecumseh, a Shawnee leader, and other tribes attacked white settlers in the Ohio Valley.	C. The Continental Army defeated the British in the American Revolution.	A. British troops would not withdraw from American forts.	D. Spain was worried about American interference in its territories in North America.

7. **B** As a strict constructionist, Jefferson would not have proceeded with any activity that was not specifically given to him in the Constitution.

8. **D** Jefferson pushed past his own concerns in order to provide for a growing nation, both in land and natural resources.

9. **A** After the Louisiana Purchase, Jefferson commissioned the Lewis and Clark Expedition to learn more about the new territory.

10. **A** One of the positive outcomes of winning the War of 1812 was a strong feeling of American nationalism.

11. Congressmen who pushed for war with Great Britain were referred to as _____**War Hawks**_____.

12. General _____**Jackson**_____ rose to national prominence following his victory at the Battle of New Orleans.

13. **D** Manifest Destiny was the belief that Americans were destined to settle all of North America from the Atlantic Ocean to the Pacific Ocean.

Answer Key

14. **C**   The concept of Manifest Destiny drove the United States to acquire new territories; the United States annexed Texas in 1848.

15. **B**   Under the justification of Manifest Destiny, American settlers pressured the US government to take over Native American lands.

Lesson 3.3

1. **D**   Because each state is represented by two Senators, the addition of a new slave state would upset the balance between free and slave states in the Senate.

2. **B**   To preserve the balance between slave and free states in the Senate, Maine was admitted to the Union at the same time as Missouri.

3. **A**   People who were opposed to slavery were known as abolitionists.

4. **C**   Because the plantation system relied on the labor of enslaved people, wealthy planters would be most likely to support the expansion of slavery.

5. **B**   When Lincoln gave his address, there were still some slave states that stayed in the Union, and Lincoln did not want to alienate them by attacking the slave states that had seceded.

6. **D**   Lincoln used persuasive language to try to convince the Confederate states to rejoin the Union.

7. **A**   A little more than a month after Lincoln delivered this address, Confederate forces attacked Union troops at Fort Sumter.

8.

North	South
More factories and materials	Familiarity with battlegrounds
More men of military age	Only needed to fight to a draw
More railroads and banks	
Naval superiority	

9. Student paragraphs will differ, but should use logical reasoning to support their predictions.

10.

Conditions for Re-Admittance to the Union
B. States would have to write new constitutions that repealed secession rights.
C. The states would have to ratify the 13th Amendment.
E. Formerly enslaved people would not be included in any provisions of the plan.

11. **A**   The Thirteenth Amendment abolished slavery in the United States.

12. **B**   Southern governments instituted black codes to limit the rights of African Americans following the Civil War.

13. **C**   By the 1870's, economic concerns had caused many Northerners to abandon the cause of Reconstruction.

Lesson 3.4

1. **B**   Most European immigrants during this period settled in east coast cities.

2. **A** Because of the large influx of Southern and Eastern Europeans during this period, cities in the northeast became overcrowded.

3. 243,860

4.

Push Factors	Pull Factors
Religious Intolerance	Democracy
Poverty	Religious Freedom
Political Oppression	Economic Opportunity

5. Student responses will vary, but should reflect an understanding of population changes in America from 1820-1920.

6. **D** Because it describes cramped, unsanitary conditions, this passage is most likely about life in a tenement house.

7. **B** In crowded tenement houses, poor sanitation often led to outbreaks of disease.

8. To combat the problems described in this passage, some reformers created _____settlement houses_____, which offered a variety of services that helped poor immigrants.

9. **Social Class Divisions**

Upper Class	Middle Class	Lower Class
Lived in city centers	Lived in neighborhoods on the edge of cities	Settled with others of the same ethnic group
Owned horses and carriages	Commuted to places of work downtown	Lived farthest from the city center

10. **D** Nativists were native-born American citizens who were fearful of increased immigration.

11. **A** Immigrants from southern and eastern Europe had religious and cultural traditions that differed from those of many native-born Americans.

12. **B** The Chinese Exclusion Act of 1882 placed extreme limits on the number of Asians who could enter the United States.

13. 300,000

Lesson 4.1

1. **D** The value of concern for lives and property after the sinking of the battleship USS *Maine* was the deciding factor in the decision made by the United States to enter the war.

2. **C** To support its new position in the world, the United States increased the size and strength of its navy.

3. **C** Because Serbia was closely allied with Russia, when Austria-Hungary declared war on Serbia, Russia and its allies entered the conflict.

4. **A** Austria-Hungary was involved in a wider _____alliance_____, or group of countries joined together by a common cause, with Germany and the Ottoman Empire.

5. **C** This passage was most likely taken from the _____Zimmermann Telegram_____.

2014 GED® Test Exercise Book

Answer Key

6. **B**   The United States had longstanding ties to France and Great Britain, but many German and Irish Americans favored the Central Powers.

7. **D**   Germany's policy of unrestricted submarine warfare, coupled with the release of the Zimmermann Telegram, caused Congress to declare war on Germany.

8. **B**   Until Russia withdrew from the war in 1918, Germany was forced to fight a war on two different fronts.

9. **C**   Germany

10. **D**   After Russia withdrew from the war, Germany was able to concentrate all its forces on its Western front.

11. In this address, President Wilson was most likely expressing his support for the creation of the __League of Nations__.

12. **C**   The Senate rejected the treaty because some senators believed the League of Nations would reduce US sovereignty.

13. Student responses will vary, but should reflect an understanding of changing attitudes toward neutrality.

Lesson 4.2

1. **D**   After being made chancellor, Hitler suspended the constitution, and therefore did not need the approval of the legislature to act.

2. **B**   Referring to the conditions of the Treaty of Versailles as "shackles" is an example of bias because it shows only one side of an issue.

3.

Germany	Italy	Russia
National Socialist Party	Seized Ethiopia in 1935	Josef Stalin
Took Czechoslovakia in 1939	Mussolini	Communism
	Fascism	

4. **C**   In 1941, Hitler added the nations of the Balkans to his growing empire.

5. **D**   Because he is referring to embarking on a "Great Crusade" in 1944, we can conclude that Eisenhower is speaking before D-Day.

6. **A**   The discovery of Nazi concentration camps, where millions of Jews were murdered, proved that the Allies were not just fighting an enemy, but were eradicating a great evil.

7. **B**   By acknowledging the strength of the enemy, Eisenhower is taking a somewhat unbiased approach to his subject.

8. **B**   FDR used few descriptive or inflammatory words in the entire speech, because he depended on the raw facts to make his case—that Japan was attacking one place after another after destroying Pearl Harbor at such a high cost of lives.

9. **A**   The United States demanded their unconditional surrender as the only acceptable end to the war with Japan, even at the cost of dropping atomic bombs on their country.

10.

Events of 1945

Cause	Effect
Allied troops surround Germany and head toward Berlin	C
President Roosevelt dies unexpectedly.	B
The Germans surrender.	E
Japan refuses to surrender unconditionally.	A
A second bomb is dropped on Nagasaki.	D

11. **D** This order, which in effect classified the West Coast as a war zone, was targeted mainly at Japanese Americans.

12. **B** As a result of this order, thousands of Japanese Americans were forced into internment camps.

Lesson 4.3

1. **B** After the war, Germany was divided into four zones, each occupied by one of the Allied nations. The zone occupied by the Soviet Union became communist and was ideologically separated from the western areas.

2. **D** The "iron curtain" countries are shaded in dark gray on this map.

3. **A** Berlin was deep in Soviet-controlled territory and could be used as a pawn in the Soviet Union's games against the West. The Berlin Blockade of 1948 is an example of how the USSR used this geography as a power play.

4. **D** The waterways into West Germany from the North Sea were important for shipping goods into West Germany, and having Denmark aligned with the United States and Great Britain meant that those lanes would remain open.

5. **C** Under a policy of containment, the United States sought to slow the expansion of the Soviet Union's influence, rather than face the Soviet Union in open conflict.

6. **B** Under the Marshall Plan, the United States provided "guidance" and security to the nations of western Europe in the form of economic aid.

7.

International Crises		
Truman	Berlin Blockade	airlifted supplies into Berlin
Kennedy	East German Crisis	increased defense spending built bomb shelters across the United States sent troops to West Berlin

8. **A** The North Atlantic Treaty Organization was created to stop Soviet expansion in Europe.

Answer Key

9. Following the communist takeover of Cuba in 1959, thousands of _____**refugees**_____ fled to the United States.

10. **D**   Kennedy's refusal to provide air support for the Bay of Pigs invasion contributed to the failure of the United States–backed rebellion in Cuba.

11. **C**   President Johnson tried to stop the spread of communism in Southeast Asia by sending troops to South Vietnam.

12. Student responses will vary, but should be supported with facts.

Lesson 4.4

1. **C**   According to the speech, the Great Society is "a place where man can renew contact with nature."

2. **A**   According to the speech, the Great Society "demands an end to poverty and racial injustice."

3.
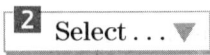
   B. Republican

   D. Paris Peace Accord

   [2] Select... ▼
   B. 1968

   [4] Select... ▼
   A. Vietnam War

4. **B**   Secret negotiations led by Henry Kissinger led to the announcement of President Nixon's visit to China.

5. **D**   President Nixon visited both nations in 1972.

6. **A**   The Watergate affair was considered to be a scandal because many people thought it was legally and morally wrong.

7. **C**   Only the initial break-in appears to have occurred, as Nixon feels free to turn his attention to other matters instead of defending himself.

8. **D**   Nixon states that US and Soviet negotiators are meeting to limit nuclear arms and to reduce the threat of nuclear war.

9. **A**   Nixon's visit to China in 1972 ended a twenty-five year silence between the two nations and helped ease tensions in the Cold War.

10. **A**   détente

11. **B**   Nixon's visit to China ended twenty-five years of diplomatic silence between the United States and China. A previous answer reveals that Nixon's China visit was in 1972. Subtract 25 years from that and 1940s is the only possible answer.

12. **A**   Democracy in Eastern Europe followed the fall of the Berlin Wall and the unification of Germany.

Lesson 4.5

1.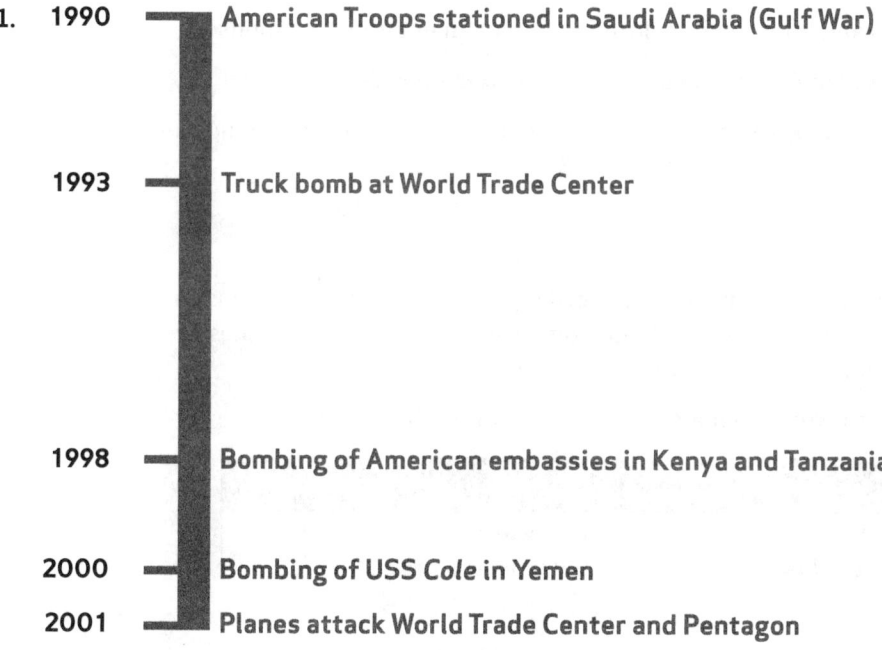

2. **C** Following the attacks on the World Trade Center and Pentagon, the United States led a coalition force that overthrew the Taliban government in Afghanistan.

3. **D** Bush states that the attacks were against the American way of life and its freedom and opportunity.

4. **C** Terrorism is a political strategy that uses violence against people or property to achieve a goal.

5. **C** The fourth plane crashed in rural Pennsylvania.

6. **D** The 2001 terrorist attacks led to the creation of the Department of Homeland Security.

7.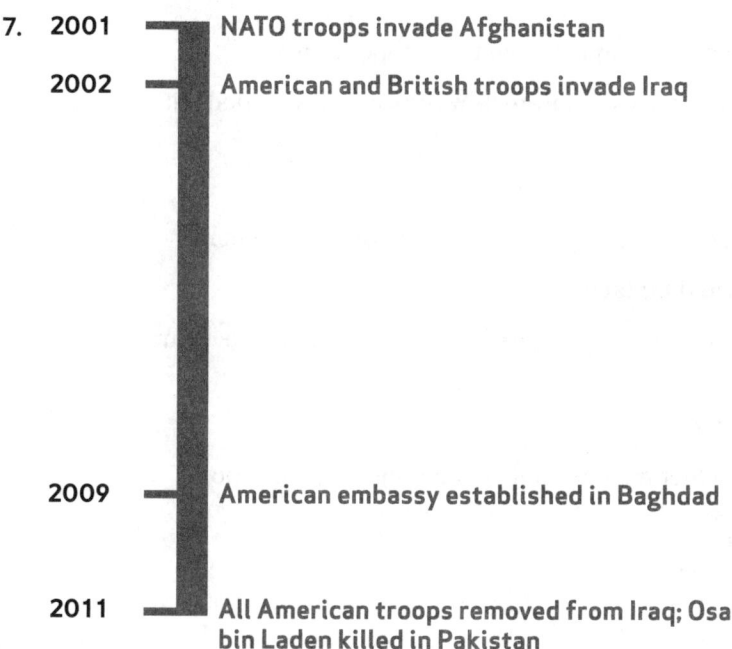

8. **A** This timeline shows how the terrorist attacks affected US foreign policy.

Answer Key

9. **C** Because he identifies hostile actions committed by the Iraqi government, it is most likely that President Bush was arguing in favor of invading Iraq.
10. **B** Sentence 5 uses imagery of mothers and their dead children to evoke an emotional response.
11. **D** The claim that Iraq has "something to hide" is vague and cannot be fact-checked.
12. **D** This term is a device to persuade others to join the US against countries it perceives as dangerous around the world.

Lesson 5.1

1. **A** A market is a place where goods and services are exchanged. This occurs at a golf course with members paying for the opportunity to play golf or to take golf lessons. Goods and services are not exchanged in a forest preserve, a classroom, or an aircraft carrier.
2. **D** The invention of money thousands of years ago made trading easier than barter.
3.

Goods	Services	Goods and Services
milk	dry cleaning	city water
washing machine	mowing the lawn	a decorated cake

4. **D** Economic systems answer three questions: what goods and services to produce, how to produce them, and for whom to produce them.
5. **A** In a market economy, price of products determines how products are distributed among the population.
6. **C** The ad shows services the restaurant provides that sets it apart from the competition.
7. **A** Smith says that both the buyer and seller serve their own self-interest. When each is satisfied with the bargain, the transaction is made.
8. **D** Self-interest is the motivation for every transaction, not benevolence.
9. **C** Competition forces sellers to lower prices or improve customer service to win over customers.
10. Answers will vary but should contain opinions supported by facts.
11. **D** A copyright protects a work of art from being reproduced or imitated just as a patent protects an inventor's new product from being copied.
12. **A** Both laws are intended to keep markets competitive.
13. **B** In a monopoly, consumers are forced to buy a product from a single company, as there is no competition from other companies.
14. **D** Trust is another term for a monopoly.

Lesson 5.2

1. **C** Scarcity is the combination of a product having value and it being in shorter supply than the number of people who want to own it.
2. **B** When the quantity of a product is greater than the demand for it, the price usually goes down.
3. **A** You gave up dinner at the restaurant in exchange for the better phone, so that was what it "cost" you to make that decision.
4. **C** Even though you needed a new cell phone, you wanted the more expensive one more than you wanted to take your friend to dinner at a restaurant.
5. **D** The four factors of production are human resources, natural resources, capital, and entrepreneurship.
6. **D** Entrepreneurship requires human creativity to succeed.
7. **B** The main factor Samuel Colt changed was how he used his labor, making their work more efficient.
8. **C** By focusing on one or two repeated skills, each worker could perfect and become faster at that skill, and the combined effort would result in a better revolver made in less time.
9. With Colt's method, more __products__ could be made with fewer workers.
10. The name for the working method developed by Samuel Colt is __mass production__.
11.

Resource	Renewable	Nonrenewable
Grains	✓	
Natural gas		✓
Cotton	✓	
Paper	✓	
Coal		✓
Land		✓

12. **B** Capital resources, labor, and production quality were all affected by the introduction of the channel wrapper.
13. **D** If the raw materials needed to create a product are unavailable or in short supply, the manufacturer may find a replacement material in order to continue production.
14. **B** When an industry has dominated a region for more than a generation, the workforce tends to develop and support those skills needed for that industry rather than developing, valuing, and supporting other skills needed for industries not found in that region.
15. **C** The mid-west and the northeast have the lowest rates.

Lesson 5.3

1. **A** Profit is money earned after expenses are paid.
2. **C** Increasing capital and other resources would boost current productivity.

Answer Key

3. **C** Business expenses include any money the company must spend, such as wages, interest payments, tools, office supplies, packaging, and utilities.
4. **D** An entrepreneur is someone who uses their creativity to develop new products.
5. According to the chart, the worst year for new housing units started was in __2009__.
6. **A** Housing sales drop during recessions.
7. **D** 1995 was a good year for home builders because the number of people buying new homes was rising.
8. **D** Production will drop temporarily when a company trains workers, buys new tools and equipment, and invests in research and development.
9. **C** Research, employee training, and new technology all help productivity. Decreasing capital investments would lead to a decrease in productivity.
10. **C** Most of the top firms in the list are pharmaceutical companies.
11. **A** Spending money on research and development can make profits for companies.
12. **A** Incentives are the offers given in a free market economy that encourage consumers to use or invent new products.
13. **B** Because traditional economies change little from generation to generation, they are only found in the most remote regions.
14. **D** The US government cannot take away a citizen's private property without proper compensation.
15. By the end of the twentieth century, several countries that had __command__ economies began to offer more free market incentives. Russia, China, and India opened opportunities for individuals to own businesses. Only a few primarily command economies remained, including North Korea, Cuba, and Iran. Increased economic freedom and opportunity gave people __incentives__ to produce more __goods and services__. Workers contributed more because they were rewarded for it. As a result, these countries experienced __economic growth__.

Lesson 5.4

1. **A** An absolute advantage is the ability to produce a product or service using __fewer__ resources than other producers require.
2. **D** Today, Americans specialize by working in one type of career field. For example, they do not tan their own leather; they buy it from someone else who does that.
3. **B** Farmers in Idaho can produce potatoes using fewer resources than farmers in other states.
4. **B** To be efficient, farmers must be able to produce desired results without wasting material, time, or energy.
5. [Select ... ▼]

    C. Absolute advantage

    [Select ... ▼]

    B. specialize
6. **C** Those with the lower opportunity cost should specialize in a product or service even if they do not have an absolute advantage.
7. **A** Look at 0 butter on the x-axis and find where the curve intersects the y-axis. This is at 50 guns.

8. **D** Look at each data point on the curve and follow it down to the *x*-axis to find out how much butter can be produced. Then following it left to the *y*-axis to see how many guns can be produced. Add both numbers together. The highest combination of guns and butter is greater than 70.

9. **D** By specializing and producing those items for which they had a comparative advantage, separate gun producers and butter producers could together produce ___120___ total butter and guns.

10. 30

11. **A** services

12. **D** Events in one country can affect events in another country.

13. **C** Because a company can concentrate its resources on one specialized trade, it can increase its productivity.

Lesson 6.1

1. **C** The study of market exchanges between buyers and sellers is called ___microeconomics___.

2. **D** A rise in prices is a signal to producers that it is time to increase production. It has a different meaning for consumers. To consumers, it is a signal to buy fewer goods.

3.

demand	The amount of goods and services buyers are willing and able to buy
mixed economy	Government regulation of parts of the market
prices	A signal to buyers and sellers
supply	The amount of goods and services a producer is willing and able to produce
command economy	Government control of the market

4. **C** Price increases are a signal to increase production.

5. **B** Price decreases are a signal to decrease production.

6. **A** The quantity demanded would be 3. Look at the *y*-axis, then draw a line to the curve and then down to the *x*-axis. This point on the *x*-axis is the quantity of CDs sold at $9.

7. 8

8. **D** The increased quantity of CDs sold when the price changed from $6 to $3 is three, which is a larger amount than any other price change.

9. 6

10. **C** Profits influence supplier decisions.

Answer Key

11.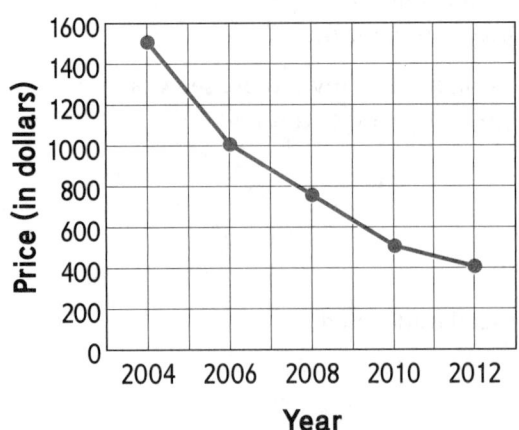
Price of 40" LED Televisions

12. The demand curve relates to the __buyer__.
    The supply curve relates to the __seller__.
    A consumer is also known as the __buyer__.
    A producer is also known as the __seller__.

13. **D** Market equilibrium is reached when demand equals the quantity supplied.

14. **B** At 600 million, the supply and demand curves meet.

Lesson 6.2

1. **C** Half of the US government's revenue comes from income taxes.
2. **B** When you buy a savings bond, you are loaning the government money to use on projects or services.
3. **C** The government borrows money by selling bonds and other securities to individuals and businesses. When you buy a savings bond, you are __loaning__ the government money.
4. **C** Subsidies are payments to the producer or consumer of a local good or service, which results in lower production costs and lower cost for consumers.
5.
| 1. Medicare/Medicaid |
| 2. Defense |
| 3. Social Security |
| 4. Nondefense |
| 5. Interest |

6. **B** In 2011, the national deficit reached $1.5 trillion.
7. **C** Tariffs are taxes on __imports__.
8. **A** Governments use __quotas__ to limit the amount of goods that can be brought into a country during a specific period.

9.

Policy	Purpose
provide a subsidy	to promote a particular business
increase interest rates	to slow economic activity or reduce inflation
enact a tariff	to American businesses from foreign competition
put money into circulation	to promote economic growth

10. **D** The Federal Reserve Act was enacted to help stabilize the US economy.

11. **B** The term *market failures* has a specific definition. It does not refer to economic problems that result from policy.

12. **D** The Federal Reserve works to preserve and maintain the financial stability of the United States.

13. **A** The Federal Reserve has many ways to increase or decrease the supply of money.

14. **B** The Fed's policies emphasize controlling inflation.

Lesson 6.3

1. **D** Gross domestic product (GDP) is the dollar value of all final goods and services produced in a country during a single year.

2. **A** Bartering is not counted in GDP, so the GDP of this nation would give an inaccurate picture of the strength of this nation's economy.

3. **C** The GDP of Mexico is $1.2 trillion and the GDP of the United Kingdom is twice that at $2.4 trillion.

4.

Part of US GDP	NOT Part of US GDP
Oil from Alaska used in Texas	Natural gas from Canada used in Illinois
Corn from Iowa sold at the Iowa State Fair	California surfboards sold in Mexico
United States-made snow tires sold separately from a vehicle in San Diego	Seats made in the United States, to be installed in a new Buick in Detroit
Automobiles designed in Japan but produced in South Carolina	Housekeeping performed by a United States homeowner

5. **B** Inflation is a rise in the general level of prices over time.

6. 40

7. **B** Prices fell between 1923 and 1933.

8. **D** The price would rise more than 2 percent because of the cumulative rates over the 10-year period.

9. **D** The ____unemployment____ rate is the percentage of individuals in the civilian labor force who are actively looking for a job but cannot find one.

10. **A** Businesses lay off workers during recession and hire them back in good times, causing ____cyclical____ unemployment.

11. **B** Unemployment appeared to reach a high of 10 percent at the end of 2009.

12. 10

2014 GED® Test Exercise Book

Answer Key

10. **D**   The Federal Reserve Act was enacted to help stabilize the US economy.
11. **B**   The term *market failures* has a specific definition. It does not refer to economic problems that result from policy.
12. **D**   The Federal Reserve works to preserve and maintain the financial stability of the United States.
13. **A**   The Federal Reserve has many ways to increase or decrease the supply of money.
14. **B**   The Fed's policies emphasize controlling inflation.

Lesson 6.3

1. **D**   Gross domestic product (GDP) is the dollar value of all final goods and services produced in a country during a single year.
2. **A**   Bartering is not counted in GDP, so the GDP of this nation would give an inaccurate picture of the strength of this nation's economy.
3. **C**   The GDP of Mexico is $1.2 trillion and the GDP of the United Kingdom is twice that at $2.4 trillion.
4.

Part of US GDP	NOT Part of US GDP
Oil from Alaska used in Texas	Natural gas from Canada used in Illinois
Corn from Iowa sold at the Iowa State Fair	California surfboards sold in Mexico
United States-made snow tires sold separately from a vehicle in San Diego	Seats made in the United States, to be installed in a new Buick in Detroit
Automobiles designed in Japan but produced in South Carolina	Housekeeping performed by a United States homeowner

5. **B**   Inflation is a rise in the general level of prices over time.
6. 40
7. **B**   Prices fell between 1923 and 1933.
8. **D**   The price would rise more than 2 percent because of the cumulative rates over the 10-year period.
9. **D**   The ___unemployment___ rate is the percentage of individuals in the civilian labor force who are actively looking for a job but cannot find one.
10. **A**   Businesses lay off workers during recession and hire them back in good times, causing ___cyclical___ unemployment.
11. **B**   Unemployment appeared to reach a high of 10 percent at the end of 2009.
12. 10
13. **A**   Unemployment was close to 6 percent at the beginning of 2003 and close to 8 percent at the beginning of 2013.
14. 8

Lesson 7.1

1. Businesses hire workers during an economic ___boom___, and the economy can experience ___expansion___. Businesses lose money and lay off workers during an economic ___bust___. During a low point in the business cycle, the economy can experience ___recession___.
2. **B**   Mass production of the Model T cut its price to 1/3 of the cost before mass production.

3. A A drop in supply when demand is high can lead to price increases.

4. B The years 1920 to 1929 would be considered a time of economic _____boom_____ in the United States.

5. Wealth in the 1920s was mainly based on the value of _____investments_____. When people bought stock, they bought it on _____margin_____, paying only about 10% and borrowing the rest. When the stock market plummeted on _____Black Tuesday_____, many investors lost all their savings. Other citizens lost savings when _____banks_____ failed.

6. B Large shantytowns populated by the unemployed and homeless appeared as a result of the _____Great Depression_____.

7. D President Hoover presided over the government as the Great Depression worsened with no relief during the early 1930s.

8. D The Great Depression was so severe that it would have taken a long time for relief programs to help all of those who were poor and homeless.

9.

Program	Description
Agricultural Adjustment Administration (AAA)	Paid farmers to produce fewer crops
Civilian Conservation Corps (CCC)	Hired people to plant forests
Fair Labor Standards Act (FLSA)	Insured money people deposited in banks
National Recovery Administration (NRA)	Regulated how much businesses could produce
Tennessee Valley Authority (TVA)	Built dams and power plants in the South
Works Progress Administration (WPA)	Hired people to complete construction projects

10. C Social Security is a form of relief that provides Americans with a pension in old age.

11. New Deal programs outlined in Roosevelt's speech provided _____stimulus_____ to the economy by providing relief to workers and reforms for businesses.

12. B Roosevelt states that his primary task is to put people to work.

Lesson 7.2

1. A The speech indicates that President Calvin Coolidge had a _____laissez-faire_____ approach to government.

2. C Coolidge rejects the idea that the rich should be taxed more, and makes the point that those who are successful should not be punished for their success.

3. B Coolidge implies that it is unjust to tax rich people at a higher rate, and that they should not be punished for their prosperity. This indicates that Coolidge does not believe that the system helped certain people to become rich but that they earned it themselves.

Answer Key

4. President Franklin D. Roosevelt used the ideas of __Keynes__, a noted economist, to create the __New Deal__ plan. This plan increased __government__ involvement in all aspects of the economy. Programs managed by the government have been used since the Great Depression, during periods of __recession__.

5.

Term	Example
Annexation	Hawaii was added to the United States as a territory in 1898.
Imperialism	The United States obtains territory to build a canal in Panama.
Open Door Policy	The United States and Mexico both have the right to trade with China.
Tariff	Sugar from Brazil is taxed when it enters the United States.

6. C One root of American __imperialism__ in the late 1800s was an overabundance of American goods.

7. A She states that the will of God made her heir apparent and the grace of God made her queen.

8. B The queen considers Hawaii to be an independent nation whose rule should be in the hands of chiefs.

9. A An increase in unemployment due to disruptions in businesses could cause homelessness.

10. US Agency for International Development provides __humanitarian__ aid to improve the lives of people in foreign countries that may have been affected by war or famine.

11. A Financial aid can provide economic stability, which can lead to political stability, which is in the best interest of US foreign policy.

12. War creates unstable __governments__, which scare away __investment__. However, money is needed after a war to rebuild __infrastructure__, to provide food and services to people who have been affected by war, and to support __businesses__ that are trying to reopen.

Lesson 7.3

1. A The __scientific method__ is the process used by scientists for testing ideas through experimentation and careful observation.

2. C During the Scientific Revolution, rational thinking caused people to question old ideas about the world and look for new answers.

3.

Solar System	Human Body
Galileo Galilei	Antonie van Leeuwenhoek
Isaac Newton	Andreas Vesalius
Nicholas Copernicus	

4. B The astrolabe allowed sailors to use the position of the sun and stars to determine the time of a celestial event, such as a sunrise or sunset.

5. C The astrolabe helped make European exploration possible.

6. C A cottage industry is one in which people work in their own homes with their own equipment and resources.

7. **C** An industrial revolution shifts a country from farming and trading to the manufacture of goods.
8. **D** In the first half of the 19th century, the development of railroads helped speed the development of the Industrial Revolution in England.
9. **C** The Industrial Revolution least affected the southwest.
10. According to the table, the cotton industry was concentrated in one area(s) of England, with two other area(s) as (a) smaller textile center(s).
11. The movement of people from farms to industrial cities appears to have been greatest in northwest England.
12. **C** Before labor unions, employers were free to treat workers according to their own company's rules.
13. **A** Industrialization affected farming, too, as new machines replaced farmworkers.
14. **D** Only the youngest children would likely be able to fit under running machines.
15. **A** Poverty most likely forced families to send their children to work in factories.

Lesson 8.1

1. **D**
2. **A** Reserves are the deposits that a bank keeps in its vaults, rather than lending back out to other patrons.
3.

credit unions	Provide emergency loans for its members
savings and loan associations	Help individuals buy homes
commercial banks	Serve the needs of business

4. **A** In the past, different banks offered different types of services, but now most offer the same services.
5. **C** Banks advertise that they have insurance to honor their promises to return deposits, if necessary.
6. **A** Banks earn a profit by charging more to borrow money than they pay to savers.
7. **D** Credit unions are financial institutions that serve members connected by a common entity.
8. **A** Checks are payable on demand, which means the bank must pay it immediately.
9. **D** Having a personal checking account allows you to withdraw money using an ATM and to write checks.
10. **C** The bank and the institution that received the check might charge a fee.
11. **A** All banks are required to protect the privacy of their depositors.
12. **A** Banks keep money safe and our privacy protected by requiring a form of identification.
13. **C** Reserve is money that a bank sets aside so they have access to it when customers ask for a withdrawal.
14. **B**
15. **B** The previous check written from this account was number ___1935___.
16. **B** To be cashed or deposited, checks must be endorsed by the person to whom they are issued.

Answer Key

17. Student opinions will differ, but should be supported by facts.

Lesson 8.2

1. **A** Credit card companies make money by charging fees and interest on monthly debt.

2.

Credit card	small purchases	highest interest rate
Installment loan	new car	paid over a specific period of time
Secured loan	home equity loan	lowest interest rate

3. **B** If the borrower defaults on a secured loan, then the lender assumes ownership of the asset or property that secured the loan.

4. **A** A ____credit score____ is a report by a credit agency of how consistently you pay your bills.

5. **D** Falling behind on loan or credit card payments can reduce a person's credit score.

6. **C** Credit agencies get their information from banks and credit card companies.

7. **B** If the interest on a secured loan, such as a home equity loan, is tax deductible, then it can help reduce your taxes.

8.

1 Harriet gets her first credit card.
2 Harriet gradually builds up her credit card balance.
3 Harriet misses two credit card payments.
4 Harriet's credit score drops.
5 A lender refuses to finance Harriet's used car purchase.

9. **D** High interest, declining property values, and an unreliable source of income should be red flags to home buyers.

10. **A** Legally, you have a right to look at your credit report once each year.

11. **A** According to the information in the passage, credit card debt is becoming more of a problem with each passing generation.

12. One way future credit cardholders can break this pattern is by paying off their ____balances____ each month.

Lesson 8.3

1. **A** The Fair Credit Reporting Act states that consumers have a right to have access to their credit reports.

2. **A** The "Opt Out" provision states that consumers can choose to have their names removed from lender marketing lists.

3. **A** The Truth in Lending Act limits a consumer's ____liability____, or legal responsibility, for purchases if a credit card is stolen and used by someone else.

4. **D** The ___Equal Credit Opportunity Act___ prohibits discrimination in credit transactions based on race, religion, sex, national origin, age, or marital or economic status.

5. **C** The writer is questioning the effectiveness of the Credit CARD Act.

6. **A** The writer believes that federal credit card protection has been inadequate to deal with the problems facing cardholders.

7. **D** You would expect that for most credit cards the lowest APRs would be on ___purchases___.

8. **B** Credit card providers are prohibited from offering no-interest loans.

9. **B** The APR is the most significant feature to compare credit card offers.

10. **A** First-time credit card users should be interested in the credit ___limit___ of the card.

11. **B** Because federal law requires credit card providers to be consistent in payment dates and times, this consumer's next due date will most likely be 5/20/12.

12. **D** The Credit CARD Act requires credit card providers to be consistent in payment dates and times.

Lesson 9.1

1. **D** As shown in the map above, the Nile River became the center of a sophisticated Egyptian civilization, or a society in an advanced state of cultural development.

2. **B** The Nile's annual floodwaters made agriculture possible, and this in turn gave rise to Egyptian civilization.

3. **A** The delta is where the Nile empties into the Mediterranean Sea.

4. **C** The pharaoh ___Khufu___ was buried in the Great Pyramid of Giza.

5. **D** The Egyptian and Indian subcontinent civilizations were centered near rivers.

6. **C** The economies of ancient Egypt and the Indus River Valley were dependent on agriculture.

7. **B** The term *mandate* most likely means command.

8. **B** The Mandate of Heaven was used by the Zhou to explain their overthrow of the Shang dynasty.

9. **A** The Mandate of Heaven gave the people the right to rebel against a wicked or ineffective ruler.

10.

Egyptian	Papyrus
Chinese	Mandate of Heaven
Indus River Valley	citywide sewage system

11. **C** Unlike the governments of Egypt and China, the governments of Greece and Rome allowed ordinary citizens to participate.

12. **A** Unlike the Greeks, who participated directly in their democracy, Romans elected officials to represent them in government.

Lesson 9.2

1. **C** The Pacific Ocean serves as a border for Hawaii, Alaska, Washington, Oregon, and California.

2. **A** The borders of ten states coincide with the Mississippi River.

3. **B** The Mediterranean Sea and the Red Sea are physical boundaries because they are natural features that separate two regions from one another.

Answer Key

4. **B** Africa and Europe are separated from North and South America by the Atlantic Ocean.
5. **C** The degrees of lines of longitude increase from east to west.
6. This map shows that lines of _____longitude_____ are not referred to as "parallels" because they meet at the poles.
7. The Equator is a line of _____longitude_____.
8. The Prime Meridian is a line of _____latitude_____.
9. **C** Lines of latitude increase in value further from the equator.
10. **C** They are measured in degrees.
11. **B** The Soviet Union was created in 1922, and its borders changed when it was dissolved in 1991.
12. **A** The creation of new borders signified that Kazakhstan had become an independent nation.
13. **D** In the absence of conflict, political boundaries can be created through cooperation between nations.

Lesson 9.3

1. **C** The president wants to develop renewable sources of energy, such as wind and solar energy.
2. **A** The United States needs new sources of energy to meet the demands of its growing population.
3. **D** Resources such as oil are nonrenewable because they cannot be replaced in a short time.
4. **A** Electricity creates more greenhouse gas emissions than agriculture. Therefore, reducing it would have the biggest impact. Increasing the other items would have the opposite effect.
5. **C** Because industries were less active following World War II, there were fewer greenhouse gas emissions, which led to lower temperatures.
6. **D** Industry was less active during World War I, the Great Depression, and World War II, so there were fewer greenhouse gas emissions.
7. **A** The goal of sustainable development is that each generation ensures that there will be adequate supplies of natural resources for future generations.
8. **B** As world economies of developing countries improve, people have more money to spend on goods and services, including those that use more energy.
9. **D** Sustainable development means consumers and companies often focus on reusing and recycling resources as well as reducing their use.
10. **A** 2011 has the lowest amount of tires going into landfills, which means it had the highest percentage of tires being reused, recycled, or used as fuel.

11.

Government Policies	increasing gasoline taxes limiting offshore oil drilling subsidizing solar energy
Individual and Business Decisions	recycling materials walking to work turning out lights

12. **B** The government could influence consumer demand by providing rebates or by subsidizing the manufacturers.
13. Student paragraphs will differ, but should support their opinions with facts.

Lesson 10.1

1.

Landform	Description
peninsula	Strip of land surrounded by water on thee sides
plain	Large area of flat land, without trees
isthmus	Narrow strip of land between two land masses, water on each side
plateau	Flat land that is raised above surrounding land surface

2. A All living organisms on Earth live on the layer known as the crust.
3. C The outer core is made of liquid metal, and the inner core is made of solid metal.
4. A The Earth's thickest layer, its mantle, is made of solid rock.
5. D Soil, minerals, water, animals, and plants are natural resources that are distributed unevenly across the Earth.
6. B All countries combined produce about 15,000 metric tons, so Chile produces about one-third of the world's copper.
7. C North and South America have three countries that are among the world's leading producers.
8.

forest	Mosses, birds, wolves, fungi, squirrels
grassland	Coyotes, hawks, bumblebees, rodents
desert	Iguana, kangaroo rat, prickly pear cactus, armadillo lizard
lake	Algae, reeds, duckweed, mollusks

9. B Areas closer to the Equator (the north in Australia) have a more tropical climate than those farther from it.
10. A The desert is less than half the size of Australia.

Lesson 10.2

1.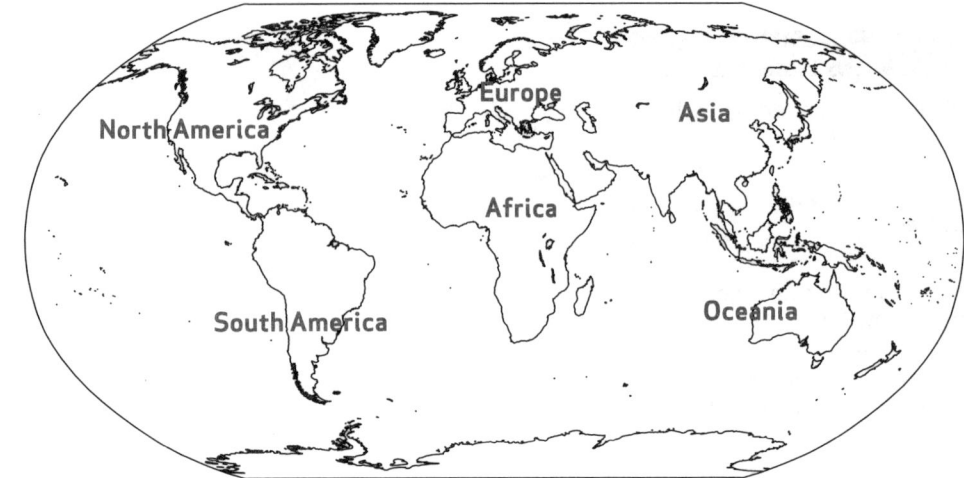

2. **C** All five bodies make up a continuous global ocean.

3.
Tropical wet	near Equator and bordered by Pacific Ocean
Arid, desert	interior Australia surrounded by mountains
Subarctic, tundra	60 degrees north latitude
Humid continental	interior region visited by storms and cloudy days
Marine, West Coast	frequent mild wet winds from Pacific or Atlantic

4. **C** There will be more rain on the eastern side of the mountains if the wind blows from west to east.

5. **A** Rainfall and warm climates contribute to a greater density and diversity of plant and animal life.

6. **B** Mandarin is the most commonly spoken language in the world.

7. **B** Regions with many cultures are considered multicultural.

8.
Indo-European languages	French, Sanskrit, Greek, Italian, English

9. **D** Large numbers of Germans, English, Africans, and Irish migrated to America between 1607 and 1820.

10. **B** If you have a diverse ancestry, you cannot accurately report it to the Census Bureau.

11. **B** The growth of residential areas and businesses into outlying areas is known as urban sprawl.

12.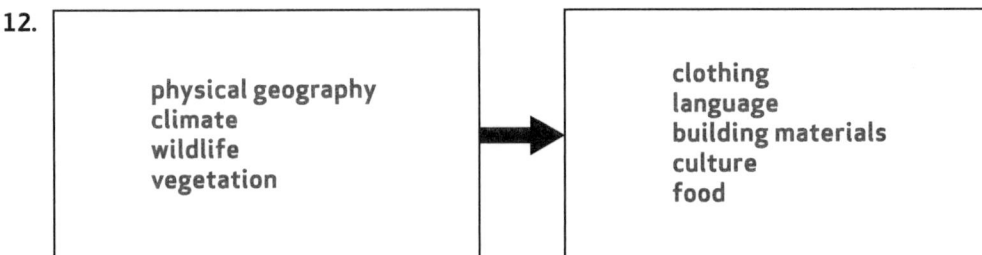

Lesson 10.3

1. **D** Nevada surpassed 30 percent growth, so there is probably a need for increased government services there.

2. A   Michigan had a negative growth in population.
3. C   Demographic information includes a population's fertility rate and mortality rate, or death rate.
4. B   The government uses census data in part to determine where new government services might be needed.
5. B   Many Europeans migrated to North America to avoid war, food shortages, and religious and political persecution.
6. D   In the late twentieth century, about 12 million people from Mexico and Asia moved to the United States, largely because of persecution and poor economic conditions.
7. B   Generally, a high fertility rate and a low mortality rate indicates a growing population.
8. B   Cultural diffusion is the spreading of cultural traits from one part of the world to another.
9. A   Buffalo presents an example of urban sprawl because its urban areas have spread into the outlying areas.
10. C   These are part of the Buffalo Metropolitan Area.

11.

1800–1850	People move from farms to cities for employment.
1870–1950	Immigrants swell the population of American cities.
1950–1980	Many city dwellers move to the suburbs just outside the cities.
1980–2010	Urban sprawl creates communities in metropolitan areas.

12. A   Over the last century, the nation of China has experienced huge population growth, a one-child policy to try to limit growth, a population shift to the coastal cities, and now an aging population.

165